Paranormal Great Lakes

An Illustrated Encyclopedia

Charles Cassady, Jr.

4880 Lower Valley Road, Atglen, Pennsylvania 19310

Other Schiffer Books by Charles Cassady, Jr.
Cleveland Ghosts, 978-0-7643-3002-5, $14.99

Other Schiffer Books on Related Subjects
Haunted Finger Lakes, 978-0-7643-3358-3, $14.99
Dayton Ghosts, 978-0-7643-3196-1, $14.99
Cincinnati Ghosts, 978-0-7643-2899-2, $14.95

Schiffer Books are available at special discounts for bulk purchases for sales promotions or premiums. Special editions, including personalized covers, corporate imprints, and excerpts can be created in large quantities for special needs. For more information contact the publisher:

Schiffer Publishing Ltd.
4880 Lower Valley Road
Atglen, PA 19310
Phone: (610) 593-1777; Fax: (610) 593-2002
E-mail: Info@schifferbooks.com

For the largest selection of fine reference books on this and related subjects, please visit our web site at:
www.schifferbooks.com
We are always looking for people to write books on new and related subjects. If you have an idea for a book please contact us at the above address.

This book may be purchased from the publisher. Include $5.00 for shipping. Please try your bookstore first. You may write for a free catalog.

In Europe, Schiffer books are distributed by
Bushwood Books
6 Marksbury Ave.
Kew Gardens
Surrey TW9 4JF England
Phone: 44 (0) 20 8392 8585; Fax: 44 (0) 20 8392 9876
E-mail: info@bushwoodbooks.co.uk
Website: www.bushwoodbooks.co.uk

Designed by Stephanie Daugherty
Type set in GrekoDeco/NewBskvll BT/Humanst521 BT

ISBN: 978-0-7643-3295-1
Printed in the United States of America

DEDICATION

For Tom Koba
Filmmaker, historian, storyteller, gone too soon.
May you find *The True Glory*.

ACKNOWLEDGMENTS

 I must thank my editors at Schiffer, Dinah Roseberry and Jennifer Marie Savage, for unearthly patience in entrusting me with this project, and the designer Stephanie Daugherty.

Other tidings of gratitude go to Rich Norgard of Alaska and T.G. Cutler, of Digital Antiquaria, for their research and advice on the convict ship Success; Frederick Stonehouse, for his inspiration and input; Carl Feindt, for his opinions on those pesky water UFOs; Robert Dean Wells in the Chicago "bureau," and ghost-trackers Sonya Horstman, Stephanie Lane, and Chuck Hawley.

Thanks to Sherry Strub, Diane Evon, John Balko, Lucy McKernan, Charles Cassady Sr., Mary Lou Cassady, David Lawson, and Sylvia Banks. Of special mention are Berni Rich, Jim Mathews, and Jeff Scott of Labwork, Cleveland's finest black-and-white custom darkroom and photo lab-studio, for generous the use of their facilities.

INTRODUCTION

When I was a boy — a strange, mostly solitary boy in the suburbs of a grey, depressed Midwestern city, where books about dinosaurs, sea serpents, ghosts, flying saucers, and everything unnatural and odd nourished my intellectual growth — I would gaze upon a map showing the Great Lakes; the shore of one of these was but a short drive away.

To me, those five swatches of blue — the **Lakes Huron**, **Superior**, **Ontario**, **Erie**, and **Michigan** — taken together looked disquietingly like thick fingers, or claws... powerful, gripping claws reaching out from the yellow ink denoting landmass...claws just behind the fine spider-webbing of a superimposed grid of latitude and longitude...as though something huge and ravenous on the other side of the map were trying to roughly pry open the US-Canadian border at the eastern end of the North American continent.

It is a purely subjective thing, I know, sort of Rorshach Test of cartography. Though in perhaps an equal stretch of the imagination one can associate my naive impression of Leviathan claws with the Ice Age glaciers that did indeed help carve the Great Lakes some 55,000 to 60,000 years ago, the receding edges of titanic talons of ice raking over slow eons of time to gouge these deep trenches in the landscape, which filled to become "inland seas" — a cluster of freshwater lakes, but above and beyond ordinary lakes. *Great lakes*... lakes so wide as to be nearly indistinguishable from the ocean. Visitors from far inland are often astounded at the expanse. Here is where twenty percent of the planet's supply of fresh water has pooled. There are few places where one can see an opposite shore at all.

They are collectively called the "Five Sisters" and many large port communities — Toronto, Milwaukee, Duluth, Detroit, Green Bay, Buffalo, Rochester, Toledo, Cleveland, and Kingston — grew and flourished on their shores. There is a Lorado Taft public sculpture, the bronze "Fountain of the Great Lakes," personifying the Five Sisters at the Art Institute of Chicago. The fountain depicts five Grecian-style women, formalized in serene, classical poses.

Given a choice between that allegory and my imaginary monster... the personality of the Great Lakes does sometimes lean towards the latter.

As shipping lanes, the Great Lakes have been said to possess many of the disadvantages of the ocean and few of the virtues. In shallower lakes, particularly Erie and Ontario, the weather can turn deadly in the short term. Only the largest of the lakes, Superior, is said to give good "freeboard," that is, room for a big ship to maneuver out of the way of a storm. Many times the "lake boats," faced with dangerous waves and wind, have had no choice but to sail into the teeth of disaster. Treacherous shoals lie off many shorelines, such as the notorious Long Point in Lake Erie or off Isle Royale in Lake Superior.

Casualty figures for the Five Sisters, then, are formidable. Approximately 6,000 vessels lost between 1870 and 1973, according to one author who did the bookkeeping. During one epic storm of November 15 to 24, 1879, no fewer than sixty-five vessels sank in the lakes, some with all hands. The deadliest Sister? That is for seasoned yachtsmen and the adjusters of maritime-insurance companies to debate. Statistically, Lake Michigan leads, her fatal reputation augmented by the atrocious casualty figures suffered in two passenger-steamer horrors: the collision between the *Lady Elgin*

and the schooner *Augusta* and the capsizing of the *Eastland* in the Chicago River.

Unlike most of the ocean, the Great Lakes can more or less ice over in the winter months. Though modern ships and icebreakers may brave the lakes in December, earlier commercial freighters, cargo ships, and schooners customarily took the month of November as a deadline for accomplishing their final hauls of the season. These voyages could be fatal gambles; the month has long exacted a fearsome toll on those desperate last runs. On Lake Ontario alone, twenty to thirty ships went down during one November storm in 1856 and, during a notorious storm in November 1913, forty ships were lost. Settlements in the isolated regions, far from the big cities, found it an ordeal to survive the winter, especially when crucial supplies were expected to come over the water.

Stories such as these now seem to belong to a remote past. Advances in lifesaving technology, search-and-rescue systems, and weather forecasting, the establishment of formal shipping lanes in 1911, and the transition from sail- and steam-powered vessels to rugged diesel-powered steel boats did much to alleviate those grim

statistics—as did, unfortunately, a changing economy. As industry died out in the Great Lakes manufacturing cities in the latter half of the twentieth century, the maritime cargo traffic also thinned. A transportation revolution represented by the family motorcar and the eighteen-wheeler truck also robbed the lake boats of their dominance. Relentless factory pollution, hunting, and over-fishing throughout much of the twentieth century threatened to murder the lakes' ecosystem. Only when man's own forests of smokestacks and sluices thinned out, curbing their own peculiar rivers of slag, smoke, and soot along the shorelines, did people realize how fragile the Great Lakes seemed.

An old engraving captures the fury of a schooner shipwreck.

Still, from time to time there is a tragedy — most recently the sudden loss of the giant freighter *Edmund Fitzgerald*, with all hands — that reminds land-dwellers that these lakes are still formidable, deep and mysterious, that those claws still reach through the map.

It is oft-repeated that the very first ship built by white men on the Great Lakes, the *Griffin*, disappeared enigmatically on her maiden voyage, vanishing with all her crew. She thus set a precedent, becoming, in legend, the first Great Lakes "ghost ship."

Superstition and strange events have bunk-mated with seamen for as long as records exist. One does not have to make a great leap of the imagination to discern that there must be something in the elemental act of voyaging across a dark, concealing expanse of water that fired the sensations and wonders of the unknown—and inspired wild tales of exotic and impossible sea creatures, horrors, and enigmas of the deep...gave rise to talismans and rituals to ward off unwanted and malevolent forces...and created taboos and cautionary folk tales about the vessels that never came back, cursed to wander beyond life and death forever; the angels and the demons of the waves; the charms and transgressions that could apportion out 'luck,' good and bad, that could save or destroy.

These superstitions go back many centuries and carry with them such archetypes of maritime lore as the Greek god Poseidon, the kraken, Jormungrad, the world-circling sea serpent, the *Flying Dutchman*, mermaids and merrows (mermen), and the Sargasso Sea, among others. Writer John Robert Columbo, a compiler of paranormal material, has commented that the unique aspect of the Great Lakes' supernatural yarns is their relatively fresh coinage. The weird lore of the open sea, like a reef, grew as the encrustation of many centuries' haphazard adventuring and travelers' tall tales, fraught with fear of the briny deep and the otherness of faraway destinations. The kindred strange narratives of the Great Lakes, for the most part, span the last two hundred years — well into the "Age of Reason" and science.

Might then these younger accounts of ghosts, curses, and creatures—unrecognized by science—be therefore, more credible? Have any of these legends of the Great Lakes proven true?

In Lake Superior, where Indian legends claimed there dwelt monsters that could upend the strongest ship, mariners claimed a "reef" existed; uncharted, a savage spire of rock just a few fathoms under the water, in a location nobody could quite determine. Most of the time, ships could pass right over it unharmed, but in intervals of especially rough seas, when the waves troughed so low this menace could almost break the surface, vessels unlucky enough to be above the thing would find their bellies fatally ripped open by the "Superior Reef."

The legend persisted, and then in 1929, it was found to be fact— forty miles off-shore was a dangerous submarine peak, rising from a depth of more than four hundred feet to just twenty-one feet below the water level. The sailors' tales were accurate. "Superior Shoal" is how the charts marked it from then onwards.

Still, the persistence of inaccuracy, lies, and foolishness, like barnacles, is a continual nuisance in the field of paranormal investigation. Sober, plain facts, like fish, become slippery and hard to hold. Not many paragraphs ago it was declared that the *Griffin* was the first ship built by white men to sail the Great Lakes and the first to come to a dire end. Not true. In fact, she was the second; the *Frontenac* was the first, pounded to pieces in the surf of Lake Ontario in 1679. But somehow the story of the *Griffin* and the circumstances of her disappearance made for a far more appealing yarn—and storytellers have christened her the first in the Great Lakes' fleet of the undead.

And it is quite a conceptual leap from something as *solid* as the Superior Shoal to ghostly ships, lighthouse poltergeists, alien spacecraft, Indian curses, or portals to other dimensions. Yet something in the human imagination snags on such rumors, even here in the hardheaded American Midwest, where water meets land and forms a boundary between the known and the unknown.

Find within these pages a veritable cargo-list of such flotsam and jetsam, presented for the benefit and fascination of the folklorist, the tourist, the occultist, the armchair adventurer, the weekend ghost-hunter, the campfire storyteller and monster-spotter, the sailor, the skeptic, and the simply curious—as I was in my youth.

As a compulsive list-maker and archivist, I have put the lore of the Five Sisters into an alphabetical order. Such encyclopedic volumes also held a childhood fascination for me. You could open them at any point, to any page and passage, and let the winds of associations blow your thoughts across the horizons like an idling sailboat.

Read these words and then look to a straightforward map of the lake chain, done by sober surveyors, and tell me if the thought doesn't strike you, how very much like claws they look.

How very much like claws...

Charles Cassady, Jr.
Seven Hills, Ohio 2008

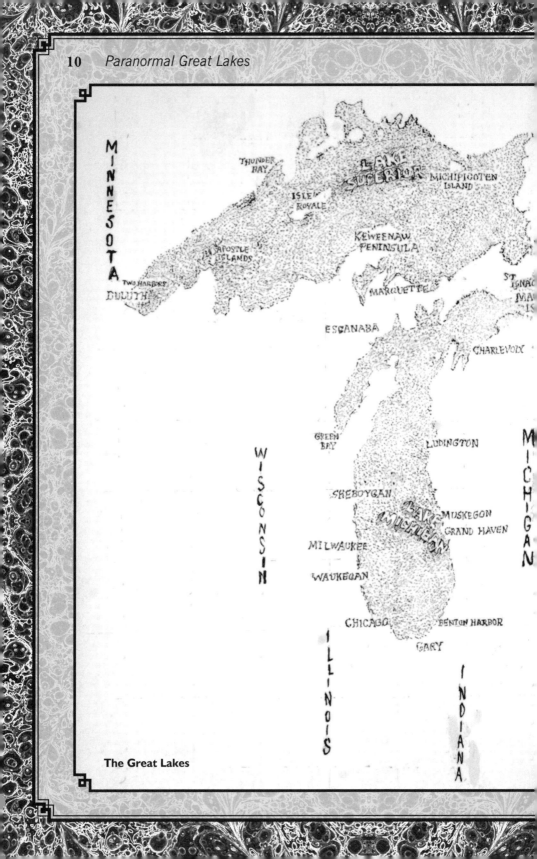

The Great Lakes

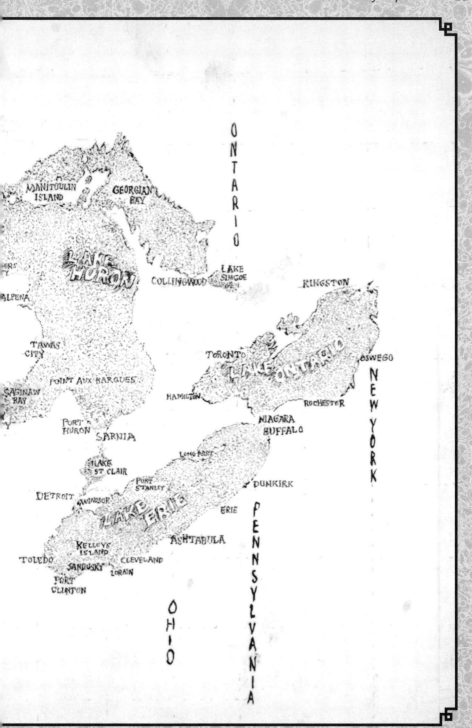

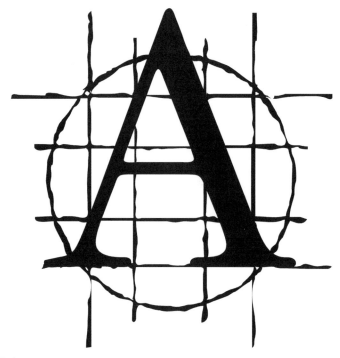

ADA (See SHIP NAMES)

ADMIRAL — A Lake Erie GHOST SHIP that began its career as the tug *W.H. Meyer* before a fateful change in name — and not only her own. For twenty years the tugboat *W.H. Meyer* operated without incident. Then she was re-registered as *ADMIRAL*. In December 1942, the *ADMIRAL* was set to sail out of Toledo for Cleveland, towing a 260-foot oil-tanker barge named the *Cleveco*. The *Cleveco* had also undergone a name change, from the original moniker of *Gotham 85* that she had carried when she was built in 1913 in Lorain.

Their double tragedy — considerably embroidered with the supernatural in recent newspaper and website retellings — is a worst-case scenario among tugboat disasters. Allegedly, before the *Admiral* and the *Cleveco* were to leave Toledo, one of the veteran hands, Joe — who was said to be clairvoyant — went into convulsions. He was replaced by a sailor with Russian-Gypsy blood and a habit of playing his violin during storms. A December storm with high winds and waves did indeed blow up. Though the beleaguered tugboat and barge maintained radio contact, it was no use. First the *Admiral* sank. Still tethered, at least for a time, to the submerged wreck, the *Cleveco* twisted helplessly in the gale while rescue boats and planes from Cleveland and Lorain encountered a chain of navigational errors, delays (including a fire on board one of their own ships), and severe weather; they were either unable to approach and conduct proper rescue operations or thrown off by an incorrectly radioed position. One cutter allegedly came within 150 feet of the stricken *Cleveco*, but could do nothing, and unusually thick snow obscured the doomed barge.

Apparently the *Cleveco* drifted...and then vanished from view—only ten miles off Cleveland—in a snowstorm. She sank with all hands, with two oil-covered corpses later found. The body of the "Gypsy" was never recovered. But a note in a bottle was and it read: "To my wife — the waves are brutal — if I die, I want you to know I love you — the violin is playing — goodbye."

To this day, sailors still report that ghosts appear where the *Cleveco* and *Admiral* went down, to dance to the Gypsy's fiddle. Or at least that is the story told, of somewhat more recent and suspect vintage. Proponents of theories that paranormal TRIANGLES and VORTICES operate in the Great Lakes have pointed to the double disappearance as evidence of a voracious, implacable predatory force at work, swallowing ships whole into some kind of limbo. These fringe theories seldom note that scuba divers located the *Admiral*, buried in silt, in 1969. In that same decade, the *Cleveco* was actually raised from the bottom and towed to deeper water, lest her oil create a slick on the already-polluted Lake Erie shores. The *Cleveco's* remaining oil was salvaged, and her wreck lies upside-down several miles off Euclid, near Cleveland. Sonar found the wreck of the *Admiral* in 1980.

ALBANY (See SHIP NAMES)

ALTADOC — A sighting recorded by Great Lakes historian Frederick Stonehouse qualifies this as a Lake Superior GHOST SHIP. She was a 365-foot Canadian steamer, bound for Fort Williams, Ontario in early December 1927, driven by a snowstorm onto rocks off the Keweenaw Peninsula, Michigan. The crew was rescued and the hulk remained fixed for decades, until salvagers cut her up for scrap during the Second World War. But while the stranded hulk still rusted on the rocks in 1932, a Lake Superior fisherman, battling a snow squall, saw a vision of the *Altadoc* ahead of him, seemingly re-enacting her final moments before running aground. The witness took that as an ill omen and gave up his fishing activities early. As the weather subsequently grew into a fierce storm, he decided that being spooked by the phantom probably saved his life. The large pilothouse of the *Altadoc* spent its own afterlife turned into a two-room hotel and gift shop until an accidental blaze destroyed it in 1987.

ANNA C MINCH (See JINXES and JONAHS)

ANNE ARBOR NO. 5 (See SHIP NAMES)

APOSTLE ISLANDS (See DEVIL'S ISLAND)

AU SABLE (See GHOST TOWNS)

AUGUSTA **and** *LADY ELGIN* — Two ships inextricably linked by tragedy, leaving the *Augusta* with the reputation as a haunted "ship-killer" schooner. Late in the summer of 1860, sailing out of Oswego, she collided on Lake Michigan with the three hundred-foot-long side-wheel steamer *Lady Elgin*. The steamer, named for the wife of the governor of Canada, had been packed with members of the Union Guards, a prominent social club for Milwaukee's Irish-American and Democratic Party community, for a day excursion to Chicago.

Though quite an attractive vessel, the *Lady Elgin* had something of a reputation of a JINX following a few mishaps in her earlier career. After nightfall on September 7, during the *Elgin's* return trip from that Chicago jaunt, and while revelers still danced on the decks, a thunderstorm began. Meanwhile the *Augusta*, carrying a load of pine and no running lights (the disposition of her lanterns would later be a subject of much inquiry), loomed out of the darkness. The schooner pierced the *Lady Elgin* at her gangplank, right beside her giant paddlewheel, soon after midnight—it was a mortal wound. Rough seas separated the two vessels, and the *Augusta*, crippled by shifted cargo but afloat, pulled into Chicago the next morning to report the accident; its captain claiming he assumed the damage to the other ship was minor. But the *Lady Elgin* was already gone. Further battered by the waves, she tried to make it to shore, but her decks collapsed and her steam-turbine engines plunged through the hole that crew and passengers vainly tried to patch with mattresses. She sank, in pieces, in thirty minutes, about ten miles from shore off Winnetka. There are horrific descriptions of onlookers seeing survivors attempting to reach shore safely; some pulling themselves exhausted onto the beach, others beaten to their deaths in the pounding surf and the wrecked pieces of decking they had used for flotation. The few lifeboats that had successfully launched also capsized before they could safely reach the beach.

In Milwaukee, the story goes that a German police officer found himself unable to sleep and felt compelled to make a house-to-house inspection of his beat — the predominantly Irish Third Ward — because of fears something terrible had happened. But the tragedy was unfolding far away. Official counts gave the number of dead at 297, but due to last-minute cancellations (because of the forecast of ominous weather) and changes to the passenger roster, the exact number of casualties has been argued. It was a stunning trauma for the Irish-Americans in both Milwaukee and Chicago. By one estimate, the accident created no less than a thousand orphaned children, and for a time this was the single worst loss of life on the Great Lakes (exceeded later by the *EASTLAND* DISASTER). Much angry finger-pointing tried to find guilt with the captains of either ship, though Captain John Wilson of the *Lady Elgin* had himself died in the sinking and was described as being heroic to the last in his efforts to save passengers, ultimately giving up his place on a floating cabin door to let others live. The official verdict — that neither ship could be held at fault — seemed to satisfy no one at all, and some historians still declare that Captain Darius Malott of the *Augusta* was made—unjustly—a scapegoat.

In later years, a vengeful throng tried to destroy the *Augusta* when she docked in Milwaukee, and the schooner's owners subsequently repainted the hull, changed her name to the *Colonel Cook*, and sold her to a New York company. She sailed in the Atlantic Ocean for a time. The GHOST legends that arose about the former *Augusta* reflect her standing as a "killer," off of which no amount of lake water could wash the bloodstains. Storytellers insisted that music could be heard playing in the *Colonel Cook*'s hull — nothing less than the band from the *Lady Elgin*, which was performing when the collision occurred. There is also a vague story that ghosts of the *Lady Elgin's* casualties tried to set fire to the *Colonel Cook*; this may be a corruption of the Milwaukee mob's attempted lynching.

Back on the Great Lakes, the *Colonel Cook* sank on Lake Erie three times in four years; each time salvaged and put back into service until a final, definitive wreck with a breakwall near Cleveland put the aging and accursed vessel out of her misery in 1894. In what many said was a case of supernatural justice, Darius Malott and nine crewmen, most of them from the *Augusta*, all vanished utterly somewhere in Lake Michigan in 1864 with their subsequent ship, the *Mojave*, close to the anniversary of the *Lady Elgin*'s demise. Details of the *Mojave*'s sinking are sketchy, so much so that other tales claim that ship too was set upon by a gang of vigilantes and destroyed as punishment.

An additional supernatural postscript claims that the spirits of the *Lady Elgin*'s dead can still be seen thrashing in the waters of Lake Michigan, trying to make for a shore. A trunk that one of *Lady Elgin*'s survivors successfully used as a makeshift raft can be seen in the museum of the Wisconsin Marine Historical Society. A piano that washed ashore off the *Lady Elgin* was also said to play itself—at the stroke of midnight every September 7.

BABY ERIE (See ERIE BABY)

BALTIC (See SHIP NAMES)

BANNOCKBURN — A 245-foot Canadian steamer lost in 1902 on Lake Superior with all hands. The suddenness of her disappearance — and stories of her being sighted later, riding storms like a veritable freshwater *Flying Dutchman* — accords the *Bannockburn* the title of "most famous" in the mythic fleet of Great Lakes GHOST SHIPS; the vessel was last seen in physical form November 21, 1902.

She was built in Scotland in 1893, at Middlesborough, and made a transatlantic crossing and passage through the Welland Canal to serve as a "canaller" lake boat for the Montreal Transportation Company. Receiving the highest rating by Lloyd's of London, she worked the sometimes-tumultuous Lake Superior without incident, casting a shadow on her name. Then, in the November of her ninth year of service, after taking on a heavy weight of Canadian grain at Port Arthur, Thunder Bay, she reportedly grounded in the harbor. An inspection turned up no damage and she was able to continue on her planned course, bound for the Sault St. Marie locks and Midland,

Ontario, in Georgian Bay. The last sighting logged has her headed towards Caribou Island, moving through a choppy lake about fifty miles southeast of Passage Island. She was spotted by another ship, the *Algonquin*, under gusty, hazy conditions.

Legend holds that Captain James McNaught of the *Algonquin* remarked to his first mate how rapidly the *Bannockburn* disappeared from view; he turned his head, and when he looked back again, she was gone...*as though swept from the face of the earth*. Indeed the *Bannockburn* and its crew of twenty, including the experienced Captain George R. Wood, were never known to come ashore again. Only one cork life preserver was found that could be traced to the ship — and this could have washed overboard previous to the ship's vanishing. Later there were rumors that, many months later, a hunter on the south shore of Lake Superior, found an oar with the ship's name cut into it, but this allegation seems dubious (in some versions of the yarn the letters spelling "B-A-N-N-O-C-K-B-U-R-N" were filled with blood!). Another steamer, the *John D. Rockefeller*, reported sighting a debris-field floating in mid-Lake Superior on November 25, but, unaware of the search for the *Bannockburn*, did not bother to investigate further.

Immediately following the ship's loss there were contradictory sightings of the *Bannockburn*, one made by the crew of the *Huronic* that she was aground near MICHIPICOTEN ISLAND. Word also circulated of her being stranded off Caribou Island twenty-two miles to the south, with all those aboard safe and sound; this account later proved heartbreakingly inaccurate to the bereaved families. The confusion may also have fed the legends, starting within just a year's time, of an often seen but vanishing vessel—the *Bannockburn* in ghostly form.

Did her grounding in the harbor wound the ship more deeply than suspected? Captain McNaught, for his part, opined that only a boiler explosion could have caused her complete and quick eradication. Wreck divers have never located the *Bannockburn* either. One detail regarding the loss that has been enfolded into the supernatural is that the lighthouse beacon on Caribou Island happened to be darkened, without explanation, on that night, potentially when the *Bannockburn* and her crew needed its guidance the most. It is this light that the ghost ship seeks when her apparition still braves the waves on storm-tossed nights.

BAVARIA (See MARYSBURGH VORTEX)

BEAVERTON BESSIE (See IGOPOGO)

BELL ROCK (See MANITOULIN ISLAND)

BELLE ISLE — An island in the Detroit River, between Detroit and Windsor, Ontario, and connected by bridge to Detroit, modern Belle Isle is a two-mile long, one-mile wide urban park of some 1,000 acres. Attached to this green space is an INDIAN LEGEND of the Ottawas that an Indian princess, daughter of Chief Sleeping Bear, was so surpassingly lovely that even the wind fell in love with her, uncovering her whenever her protective father hid her blanketed in a canoe. Thus did a brave on the shore espy her; he also became infatuated and took the girl in. The jealous wind buffeted the mortal suitor to death. Finally, Sleeping Bear put his daughter on Belle Isle, where she could run and play with the wind and not draw the troublesome attentions of men. The spirits, well pleased with this solution, granted the princess immortality and also transformed the girl into a white deer on Belle Isle.

Like many Great Lakes islands, Belle Isle served as habitat for multitudes of water snakes (it was for a time called Rattlesnake Island), and some tellings of the legend state that the serpents are there to guard this "Snake Goddess of Belle Isle" (sometimes simply "Goddess of Belle Isle"). She is still occasionally seen in human form, according to folklore, a beautiful girl in native dress suddenly present among the picnickers. (Campfire-like tales of seductive Indian "snake goddesses" recur at more than one location throughout the lakes). A more recent female GHOST associated with Belle Isle is, possibly, a co-mingling with the Indian mythology of a recent urban-legend motif. There is a traffic bridge within Belle Isle, most sources place it as the one near the southwest portion of the island, spanning a "Lake Tacoma," and if a motorist idles on the bridge, a "Lady in White"—sometimes described as old, sometimes young—will emerge from the woods and beckon to be followed.

Generations of Detroiters have attempted this ritual dare; most seeing nothing, some claiming (or bragging) to have witnessed the Lady in White — who has sisterly counterparts on bridges and cemeteries throughout Michigan, and indeed throughout the country, comporting themselves in similar fashion. Storytellers claim she was a murder victim or a suicide/accident casualty on an unhappy high school prom night. It has been pointed out that there have been sufficient suicides or homicides linked to Belle Isle or the Belle Isle Bridge to lend credence to the legend and the whispered scare-stories.

BENJAMIN NOBLE (See GHOST SHIPS)

BETE GRIS — A popular Lake Michigan beach on the Keweenaw Peninsula in Upper Michigan. A rather tourist-friendly INDIAN LEGEND is attached to Bete Gris. The story goes that a native maiden was separated from her lover across the expanse of the lake. The sands here are of a quality texture and composition so that when one presses them down and twists, the grains rubbing against each other produce a singular sound. This is said to be the girl's siren song calling to her lost love. The name of the beach translates as "Grey Beast" in French, which has seeded talk of a monstrous creature of some sort haunting the area as well. But it seems more likely the name came from a phonetic corruption of "baie de gres," or "bay of sand," in the original French tongue of the old explorers and settlers. Out of such small grains arise tall tales indeed.

BIG BAY POINT LIGHTHOUSE — A reputedly haunted lighthouse overlooking Lake Superior, the lighthouse was built in the late nineteenth century, northwest of Marquette, Michigan, on five layers of bricks mortared into the sandstone cliffs of Big Bay Point, where it now functions as a quaint bed-and-breakfast inn. The structure houses two apartments — one for the keeper, the other for the keeper's assistant — built around the square light tower, at the summit of which was a steel-railed observation deck tower. The edifice was intended to serve as a beacon for the coastline between the Huron Island and Granite Island lights.

Its principal GHOST is usually said to be the first of the keepers, William 'Big Willie' Prior, described as a former military man and exacting taskmaster, who took charge of the light when it opened in 1896. Eventually he settled on his own son, Edward, as his assistant. In 1901, however, Edward died of an infection from a leg injury suffered during his chores. He was only twenty-years-old. A few weeks later, the bereaved Big Willie disappeared. Eventually his decomposed remains were found in the woods a mile and half away, where the heartbroken father had evidently hung himself. The eighteen-room lighthouse and keeper's quarters were manned until 1941, after which the Coast Guard built a separate, automated light tower. In 1951 the US Army used the site for training an anti-aircraft battalion. During this interval, an Army officer killed a civilian tavern-owner and the defense attorney, under the pen name "Robert Traver," wrote a *roman a clef* novel *Anatomy of a Murder*, which inspired a Hollywood courtroom drama partially filmed on location at Big Bay and around

Lighthouses on the Great Lakes have become a haven for many GHOSTS...

the lighthouse. That fatal local color, however, has not fed overtly into the ghost mythos.

Beginning with its auction to the public in 1961, the Big Bay Point Lighthouse passed through a series of private owners, two of whom were Norman and Marilyn Gotschall. In the 1980s they decided to convert the much-modified structure into a bed-and-breakfast inn. Norman Gotschall first reported *otherworldly phenomena* in 1986, which included:

> • Inexplicable banging noises;
> • A cleaning woman screaming about a mysterious man seen in a shower stall, but nobody could be discovered;
> • Guests reporting the faint specter of a figure in the uniform of a lighthouse keeper, walking the grounds;
> • Another guest reported seeing a man in a military uniform with bright gold buttons standing at the foot of the bed. Before vanishing, the untypical verbose *GHOST* of Big Willie stated he was upset by all the commotion in the lighthouse and he would not be content until the renovation work concluded.

In 1990 the Gotschalls sold the lighthouse to a trio of Chicagoans, including another husband and wife team, Linda and Jeff Gamble. They received visits from so-called "psychics" who informed them that, aside from Big Willie, the Big Bay Point Lighthouse had *four other* resident ghosts; three ill-defined entities (possibly area shipwreck victims) and a female from the late 1950s. The restless young woman haunts the suites that used to be the assistant keeper quarters, while Big Willie stays around the original lighthouse and grounds with which he is most familiar. Manifestations reported by the Gambles include doors and windows closing (and locking) of their own volition, lights and radios switching off, and one guest at night looking in her room mirror and glimpsing, via flashlight illumination, a tall man in a lightkeeper's hat behind her.

Big Bay Point continues to operate as a B&B, one of only three Lake Superior lighthouses to do so.

BIG BILL (See KARSTEN INN)

BIG MCCOY ISLAND — Largest of the McCoy Islands, an island group in Georgian Bay, northwest of Parry Sound, off Ontario, the archipelago carries a vague folk legend about the otherwise nameless 'McCoy'; purportedly he was a pioneer trader of ill repute who made a home for himself on the largest island (now called Big McCoy). Further embellishments claim he was even murdered by one of his many enemies, an Indian, or a fellow white man he had swindled. Every September during a full moon, it's said, two piercing shrieks are heard from the woods on Big McCoy Island—the GHOST of McCoy, either raging at his fate or, paradoxically, exultant that he has beaten the devil in some nefarious deal.

BIG WILLIE (See BIG BAY POINT LIGHTHOUSE)

BLACK DOG OF LAKE ERIE — A ghostly OMEN that the old-time mariners would tell from the Great Lakes age of sail, the Black Dog of Lake Erie was a portent of disaster if seen padding on deck or running up and down the ship's masts. Its origin is stated in an apocryphal tale: the black dog was itself a GHOST, an unspecified ship's pet that had accidentally fallen off the deck as the vessel made passage through the Welland Canal. None of the men on board troubled themselves to try and retrieve the desperate animal from the waves, letting the unfortunate dog drown. Subsequently a gate of the canal lock seized up, and the crew strained to free the ship. When the gates finally opened, the dog's carcass was revealed, wedged in the mechanism, as though in retribution. Even after that the dog's spirit haunted the boat... its mournful howling frequently disturbing the sailors' rest.

Afterwards the Black Dog of Lake Erie appeared on other doomed ships, sometimes only visible to those sailors gifted with second sight. "May the Black Dog of Lake Erie cross your deck!" was not a curse to be taken lightly in the old days, writes Great Lakes historian Frederick Stonehouse. One shipwreck closely associated to the Black Dog legend was the sinking of the schooner *T.G. Jenkins* in November 1875, on Lake Ontario, during a passage from Chicago. As the ship crossed Lake Erie, a drunken helmsman frantically babbled about seeing the mythic hound of ill fortune scramble out of the lake and walk around the ship's decks. The man was positively in hysterics by the time the *T.G. Jenkins* went through the Welland Canal and he was put off the ship. Supposedly he ran from lock to lock, shouting from the shore to his old shipmates that they had to get off the boat if they wanted to save their lives. But the *T.G. Jenkins* continued on.

In uncertain weather, the ship disappeared near Oswego, New York, leaving no wreckage or survivors. But it's said that a New York farmer saw a disheveled black dog literally *dragging itself ashore* that same night...and then vanishing into the darkness. The captain of the *T.G. Jenkins* did own a black dog, a fairly small one, and it had been aboard for the ill-starred voyage. So the story ends on a teasing note of literary ambiguity. Did the Black Dog of Lake Erie truly cross the schooner's deck?

Black dogs are a folk archetype in many regions and cultures, especially throughout Europe, and ghostly black dogs have been reported haunting in-shore areas of Wisconsin.

BLUE BANKS — An area along the Huron River south of where it flows into Lake Erie, north of the Ohio town of Monroeville. Blue Banks is best known to mineralogists for the quantity of blue shale, exposed by water erosion, that gives the area its name, but there is also a local GHOST story. A white settler named 'Sanduski' (probably not coincidentally, the city of Sandusky is to the north) was romantically obsessed with an Indian maiden, assaulted her, and the girl fell into the river and drowned. The maiden's fiancé, a vengeful Indian brave, caught Sanduski and skinned him alive. The story concludes that the voice of the long-dead Indian maiden can still be heard singing sadly, and it's best heard if you sit on the blue banks overlooking the river.

BOILING OF THE BAY (See WEATHER ANOMALIES)

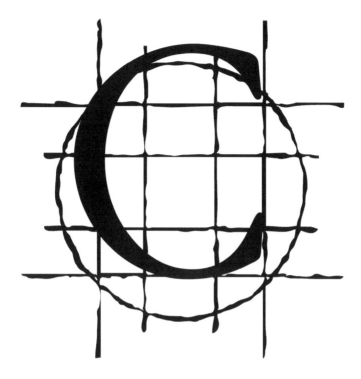

CALCUTTA (See SHIP NAMES)

CHAMBERS ISLAND LIGHTHOUSE — An 1868 lighthouse attached to a handsome keepers' home, built on Lake Michigan to guide vessels through Green Bay's western passage, the sixty-foot tower was rendered obsolete by an automated beacon in 1951, suffering vandalism afterwards. In the 1970s forty-year Coast Guard veteran Joel Blahnik convinced the town of Gibralter to preserve the lighthouse and its estate as a public park and museum. Along with his efforts to restore and renovate the scarred structure came Blahnik's account of a GHOST...never seen, but always *heard* each spring when he re-opened the door. Its heavy footsteps could be heard echoing down the tower, and other unexplained noises and vanishing tools during restoration would be blamed on the nameless spook. Manifestations ceased in 1987. A group of nuns taking a tour of Chambers Island Lighthouse were told the customary version of the haunting. One of the women laid hands on the brick tower and prayed for the release of the spirit trapped within. From then on, it is said, the Chambers Island ghost has been at peace.

CHARLES POINT — This Lake Ontario resort community (variously called Point Charles) on Sodus Bay in New York State is the scene of a moralistic GHOST report—and the yarn was enshrined in detail in a Rochester newspaper in 1921. A caretaker of the cottages, one George Carson, in clearing the area for the influx of summer visitors, thoughtlessly removed a recent tombstone marking the resting place of a French-Canadian sailor.

The dead man had been discovered drowned on the beach nearby in 1857 and was buried at Charles Point. Afterwards, the tradition claimed, moaning sounds could be heard around the lonely grave, especially when storm winds blew. In 1917, during especially fierce gusts, three cottage inhabitants heard rapping at their door at midnight, and when they went to investigate, beheld a glowing form seated on a bench outside their building. It walked over to the sailor's grave, raised two apparent 'arms,' and sank into the earth. So impressed were the witnesses that they created the marker reading:

"TO THE DEAD SAILOR BURIED HERE IN 1857."

It was this small monument that Carson had uprooted in his cleanup efforts. At 9 p.m. that night the sight of the sailor's ghost affrighted the caretaker; evidently agitated, the ghost paced between the bench and the grave, before again raising its arms and disappearing. Carson retrieved the marker from the rubbish and put it back...placating the restless spirit.

CHARLES PRICE and *REGINA* — One of the most puzzling unsolved mysteries of Lake Huron was a fluke detail of the legendary killer storm of November 11, 1913. The *Charles Price* was a 10,000-ton, 534-foot ore steamship whose assistant engineer, Milton Smith, is reported by collectors of OMENS and PROPHECIES to have refused to set off on the late-season voyage hauling nine hundred tons of coal from Ashtabula, Ohio to Superior, Wisconsin. (With 50 mph-velocity winds, his apprehension may be well understood.) The *Regina* was a 269-foot, 1,956-ton Canadian steamer, carrying a cargo of lumber. The two ships drove into a nightmarish gale, one that ultimately caused forty shipwrecks. Many have accounted it as the worst single storm to ever ravage the Great Lakes in the maritime era. The *Charles Price* was later found floating upside-down, while the *Regina* disappeared. There were no survivors from either.

Ice-encrusted corpses of the more than 230 sailors lost in the great storm of 1913 were found on shorelines along Lake Huron; some men frozen to their life preservers, others in each other's arms. It is the peculiarity of the dead from the *Charles Price* that links that ship forever with the *Regina*: As bodies from the *Price* were fished out of Huron, they were found wearing life jackets plainly identifiable as belonging not to their own vessel...but to the *Regina*. How could this be? Lakes historians have concocted varied scenarios. Perhaps the ships somehow rammed into each other or that the *Charles Price* foundered and its crew, oddly jacketless, was picked up by the *Regina*, which straightaway succumbed to the raging lake herself.

Yet the last known sightings of the two ships put them more than a dozen miles away from each other—and possibly much further. Believers in TRIANGLES and VORTICES on the Great Lakes have cited this mystery as yet another example of incomprehensible forces twisting the fabric of reality inside-out on the turbulent waters. (See also COVE ISLAND LIGHT)

CHICORA — A prominent GHOST SHIP of Lake Michigan, she was a 217-foot, 1,122-ton wooden steamer built in 1892 by the Graham & Morton Transportation Company. The well-appointed vessel was intended to run passengers and cargo between Milwaukee and St. Joseph, Michigan. In January 1895, the ship's Captain Edward Stines decided to risk the winter weather and make a final, unscheduled run for the season between the two ports, with a crew of twenty-three (including his own son as first mate) and one passenger. Stories would later circulate that on a previous trip, a duck alighted on the ship in mid-lake, and a passenger summarily shot it, dooming the *Chicora* to bad luck.

As the *Chicora* embarked on what would be her last voyage, the owner, alarmed by a rapidly falling barometer, tried to prevent her departure, but he was too late. When his wire-telegram message arrived at the dock in Milwaukee, she had already set off. Soon the temperature plummeted forty degrees and a violent storm lashed Lake Michigan. Weeks later substantial wreckage from the *Chicora* began washing ashore at Grand Haven, thirty-five miles north of St. Joseph. Yet sightings of the lost *Chicora* had come in shortly after her disappearance, placing the ship as marooned in ice—with about nineteen survivors visible—seven miles out. The stories became even more tantalizing when a dog, recognized as the ship's own mascot, was found ashore at Benton Harbor, whimpering but alive, as though it had crossed the ice on foot. Rescue boats set out for the alleged location of the stricken ship, but found nothing.

No bodies from the steamer ever turned up, though scattered accounts claim that bottle messages were found describing the crews' ordeal, trapped helplessly in the ice. One such story said a grisly relic discovered was a cloth cap from the ship's line — with a skeletal hand clutching it. The *Chicora* subsequently passed into legend, as a phantom ship sighted occasionally by Lake Michigan car ferries; the steamer visible at a distance of a few miles, sometimes blowing distress signals... and then suddenly vanishing. She would be taken as an *omen* of a dangerous approaching storm. In 2001, an expedition announced the discovery of the wreck of the *Chicora* at 260 feet off the eastern shore of southwest Lake Michigan.

CHRISTMAS TREE SHIP (See *ROUSE SIMMONS*)

CITY OF DETROIT (See *WATER WITCH*)

CITY OF CHEBOYGAN (See SHIP NAMES)

CLEVECO (See *ADMIRAL*)

COD — A heroic submarine moored at Cleveland in Lake Erie, and on display, she's said to be patrolled by a dutiful *ghost*. The *USS Cod* was one of the American fleet of World War II naval attack submarines, her keel laid by the Electric Boat Company of Groton, Connecticut, in 1942 as a response to the Pearl Harbor attacks. The diesel sub and her arsenal of twenty-four torpedoes extracted vengeance against Japan in eight patrols beginning in October 1943. She sank at least twelve enemy transports and battleships, sending 37,000 tons of the Empire of the Rising Sun to the bottom.

The *Cod* distinguished herself especially by performing history's first (and so far only) submarine-to-submarine rescue. In July 1945, it came to the aid of a Dutch sub that had run aground on a reef, taking on the fifty-six Netherlanders and raising the population of the 312-foot boat to a packed 153 people during the two-day trip to Subic Bay.

During her entire span of service, the *Cod* herself lost only one crewmember; during her sixth patrol in April 1945, the crewman had been outside and washed overboard in the confusion of a Japanese attack and a torpedo-room fire, drowning in the South Pacific as the ship took a heavy pounding from depth charges. The *Cod* survived past V-J Day, made post-war goodwill tours, and beginning in 1959, called the Great Lakes home, after being towed through the St. Lawrence Seaway to serve as a training vessel. The Navy thought of scrapping her or

A World War II submarine with a GHOST tradition, the *COD*.

using her for target practice after retirement, but former crewmen and Clevelanders who had grown fond of the *Cod* rallied to her defense. In 1976, the submarine opened to the public as a permanent memorial and museum on the lakefront. She is very likely the best-preserved and restored American World War II submarine on display.

In recent years the vessel is said to be *haunted* by the spirit of its lone fatality. Some staff members have reported feelings or sensations of being followed while in the cramped quarters of the hull. When they turn around, nobody is there. One caretaker closed early, giving the *invisible intruder* as a reason. But the ghost is not taken to be hostile—rather the drowned submariner is still looking after his ship. At least that is the interpretation given by the burgeoning local "ghost tour" industry when their buses stop at the *Cod*.

COLONEL COOK (See *AUGUSTA*)

COMET (See SHIP NAMES)

COVE ISLAND LIGHT — An elaborate and well-preserved lighthouse on northeast Lake Huron, north of the Bruce Peninsula, its eighty-five-foot tower lit the waters in 1858 after several beacons were installed on Cove Island to delineate a dangerous passage between Lake Huron and Georgian Bay. Its original name was Isle of Coves Lighthouse, but that has evolved during its long years of service. The light remains on active duty, maintained by the Coast Guard, still using its nineteenth century Fresnel lens. Another holdover at Cove Island, according to maritime lore, is a resident GHOST that acts rather like a *guardian spirit*.

Tradition holds that this is Captain Amos Tripp, of the schooner *Regina*, which sank here, laden with salt, during a gale. Captain Tripp drowned, and his body, discovered by the keeper of the light, received a makeshift burial in sailcloth on the west side of the island. Subsequently a helpful ghost—presumably Tripp's—could be glimpsed as a flitting shadow or figure on the beach keeping watch during storms. The ghost could especially be sensed as an invisible presence that completed maintenance chores of polishing mirrors and trimming wicks.

An undated, apocryphal tale claims that during a fierce November storm, sailors in the vicinity were struggling without the light's accustomed guidance. Finally it blinked on, preventing certain disaster. Only later did the keeper confess he had been absent without leave at the time—someone else had lit the beacon in the supposedly deserted tower that night. Who could it have been but the late Captain Tripp? Additional embroidery claims that the long-dead captain would, on select nights, materialize to play cards with the keepers. (See also *CHARLES PRICE* and *REGINA*)

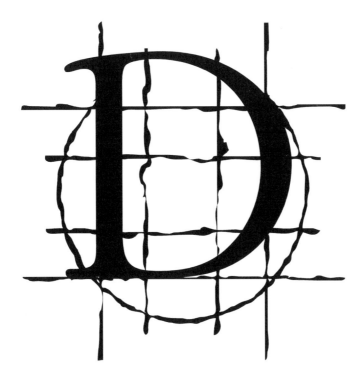

DANIEL J. MORRELL — A Lake Huron ship calamity of living memory and the worst Huron wreck in forty-two years produced a memorable survival tale—*with supernatural tinges*.

The *Daniel J. Morrell* was a nearly six hundred-foot steam-powered ore carrier, built of steel by the Bay City Shipbuilding Company of West Bay City, Michigan, launched in 1906. In 1966, she was entering her sixth decade of service on the lakes. The issue of her age and the long-term durability of steel ships will be much discussed later, as some accounts describe her as plagued with leaks and engineering senescence; others praising the old ship for solidly withstanding the one hundred-mile winds of a killer storm in 1958 (two years after she had received a new engine). On her last voyage, she was bound for Taconite Harbor, Minnesota, in November 1966, to take on a cargo of iron in a last-minute run at the end of the season. Her sister ship, the *Edward Townsend*, was making the same haul; both great ships employed by a subsidiary of Bethlehem Steel.

After a brief docking in Detroit, the *Daniel J. Morrell* resumed the journey, as Captain Arthur Crawley attempted to outmaneuver bad weather. Waves pounding the ship reached twenty-five feet and wind speeds were recorded at 65-mph. In the early hours of November 29,

1966, about two hours after final radio contact with the *Townsend*, which was fighting the same rough seas, the *Daniel J. Morrell* simply ruptured in half and sank in anywhere from eight to fifteen minutes. There was neither time nor electricity to send distress signals on the freighter's full complement of radio gear and the crew beheld a nightmarish sight—the severed stern of the ship, with the new engine still functioning and lights still blazing, propelling itself askew and away into the night. The life rafts into which Captain Crawley and most of the twenty-nine crewmembers had scrambled were tossed by both its wake and the waves.

It would take thirty-four hours for an organized emergency search-and-rescue operation, once the mainland realized, belatedly, that the *Daniel J. Morrell* was overdue. A Coast Guard helicopter, searching near POINT AUX BARQUES, nineteen miles south of where the ship sank, found a life raft from the ship and its tragic cargo — three dead men and one frostbitten, his bare legs covered with ice, but still living. The lone survivor was 26-year-old Dennis Hale, who, ironically, had nearly missed the deadly voyage due to car trouble. Awakened in his bunk by a series of bangs and wearing practically nothing but his shorts and a pea coat, Hale had watched with horror as the boat wrenched in two and had taken to the raft with his crewmates. Morrell had seen the other three men die, one by one, of exposure, internal injuries, and drowning, within fourteen hours after the sinking as the raft bobbed helplessly on icy seas, sometimes torturously within sight of land. For a full twenty-four hours he had been alone, with nothing but the company of dead men.

Or had he been alone? Admitted to a hospital with a body temperature of ninety-four degrees, Hale called for a Catholic priest to administer last rites, and he confessed what had transpired on the raft. The priest's negative reaction convinced Hale to stay quiet about the strangest aspect of his survival during the subsequent inquest, declaring later, "It was a personal matter, beyond the ken of those who had never experienced such an ordeal." Hale had spent much of his time on the corpse-strewn raft in delirium, playing mental solitaire, talking to his dead friends, praying, and cursing. But when it came to the reason he had lived through the calamity, he credited a mysterious stranger—a man in white with piercing eyes, a neat mustache, and pale/translucent skin that, on close inspection, was exceptionally wrinkled, particularly the hands and fingers. Hale would give this apparition the nickname 'Doc' when he later retold his story in full.

> "I had been thinking of hospitals, warm beds, and food when he appeared. How *he* talked to me I don't know."

'Doc' appeared twice, sternly warning Hale to stop eating the ice accumulating on his coat, no matter how hungry or thirsty he was. Minutes after his first exchange with Doc, Hale said he underwent what could be considered an "out-of-body experience," rising through a softly-spinning cloud to enter a green meadow, where he beheld a bridge, on the other side of which gathered his deceased relations, including the mother who had died not long after his birth. At a distance Hale also spotted a man with a golden crown, who never spoke to him but seemed to watch and radiate benevolence. A sort of guide, different in appearance from Doc but dressed similarly in white, welcomed Hale and allowed him to cross the bridge. When the sailor asked his relatives about the *Morrell*, he was directed over the hill to a misty valley, where he was told he could find the ship.

There indeed was the severed bow. Hale climbed the familiar ladder to the deck, where several crewmates met him with "innocent and childlike" joy (which, Hale had to note, was quite out of character for veteran lake men). Then the severed stern section appeared, and physically reconnected with the bow, making the *Morrell* whole again. Going with his crewmates to visit the engine room ("I'm not sure how we moved, as no one seemed to have any legs. We just seemed to float or glide along.") Hale was met by the ship's engineer, who protested that it wasn't Hale's time to die. Straightaway, Dennis Hale awoke back on the raft.

He called upon Doc for help, and started to eat the ice now clinging to his coat. Doc appeared for the second and final time, repeating his warning. Hale obeyed, stopped eating ice — and thus avoided fatal hypothermia. Shortly thereafter a rescue helicopter found Hale's raft.

Directly the *Edward Townsend* immediately came under intense scrutiny. Already the crew had found cracks in her hull and substantial leakage. She was taken out of service and sold for scrap on the foreign market. Most ominously, while being towed on the Atlantic Ocean to a Spanish scrap yard, the *Townsend* also broke in half. After an exhaustive inquiry (and numerous lawsuits on behalf of Dennis Hale and the *Morrell* victims resulting in the one of the largest settlements in maritime history), the National Transportation Safety Board recommended retiring vessels of such age — though, as one author pointed out, this became a moot point as recession ravaged the Great Lakes steel industry.

As for Dennis Hale, he later underwent eleven operations over the years to his cold, damaged feet. He worked subsequently as a machinist, suffering shades of survivor's guilt and trauma, and struggled through addiction and divorce. Not until 1981 did Dennis Hale begin speaking publicly about what he had undergone and the miraculous visitation of Doc and his "visit" to the *otherside*. He ultimately became a regular on the lecture circuit and curator of the Ashtabula Marine Museum. Hale has been the subject of a Great Lakes ballad, appeared as a motivational speaker, and, in 1996, published his memoir Sole *Survivor*. "I find peace in helping to keep the memories of my shipmates alive," he concludes in its pages.

Lakes historian Frederick Stonehouse has remarked that the phantom of 'Doc' is consistent with accounts of a long-lost Point Aux Barques lifesaving crew continuing work as "protective" GHOSTS.

DAUNTLESS and DEAN RICHMOND (See SHIP NAMES)

DEATH'S DOOR STRAIT (See PORTE DES MORTES)

DEVIL'S CHAIR — This rock formation, prominent in INDIAN LEGENDS, juts up through the water off Gargantua Cape, on the Canadian side of Lake Superior. It is a jagged, roughly triangular shape, with a few water-carved holes and arches. In Ojibway-Chippewa beliefs, the rock was said to have been created by the great spirit Gitchi

The rocky islands and crags of Lake Superior's "haunted shore" have sired numerous INDIAN LEGENDS such as DEVIL'S CHAIR or DEVIL'S ISLAND.
Photo copyright by Sylvia Banks.

Manitou after he made all things; indeed, the version of the legend recorded by early missionaries claim that the rock *IS* the great spirit, along with two of his favorite dogs, turned to stone once his work was completed. The grim name may well have arisen from the disdainful attitudes of the white Christian settlers, who automatically condemned any elder-spirit deity of pagan faith to be demonic. In any case, early records told of Indians leaving sacrifical offerings (such as tobacco) at the rock as a matter of routine. More modern gossip speaks of bloody human-sacrifice rituals and baneful vibrations here. Author Wayland Drew dismissed the spooky reputation as being the toxic after-effects of the Europeans' harsh prejudices against a tribal sacred place. Fortunately, Devil's Chair now sits in a protected area of the Lake Superior Provincial Park, and the pilgrims most likely to row past it now are canoe and kayak enthusiasts, not vandals and occultists.

DEVIL'S ISLAND — This island marks the northernmost part of the Apostle Island group in Lake Superior. Making landfall is a difficult chore on this rugged outcrop of sandstone, whose various layers have been worn and carved into sea cliffs and caves through the centuries. Great Lakes writers Larry and Patricia Wright describe Devil's Island as looking like worm-eaten wood, and as evidence of its relative inaccessibility, cite the fact that not until late in the era of shipping — 1891 — was a lighthouse beacon completed here, at a key waterway. The forbidding name of the island derives from INDIAN LEGEND, and in the Ojibway-Chippewa Indian tongue, the place was called "Metchimanitou Miniss," or island of the evil spirit Metchi Manitou, dark opposite of the venerated Gitchi Manitou. The tribes evidently took fright at the eerie noises, created by the surf, echoing through the island's network of sea caves. In 1928 none other than President Calvin Coolidge visited Devil's Island to behold the caves. Otherwise public visits to the island by all but the lighthouse-keepers, their suppliers, and Coast Guardsmen (who automated the beacon in 1978) have been sparse.

DIANA OF THE DUNES — This GHOST of the Lake Michigan beaches at Indiana Dunes State Park has been described as a *vanishing woman*, walking or scurrying through the sands, or furtively glimpsed by moonlight, or heard weeping. In a most distinguishing characteristic, she is sometimes said to be nude.

The actual story of Alice Mable Gray, dubbed "Diana of the Dunes" by a sensation-seeking contemporary press, has been retold, distorted, and romanticized. Picture the famous Maxfield Parrish imagery depicting an unclothed naiad on a shore, under the starlight—and one can conceive of how rumors of a wild, beautiful hermit girl living in the remote dunes by herself and swimming naked in Lake Michigan might have set typewriters flying in the nascent "flapper" era. That Gray did bathe in the lake regularly (there being no running water in her shack) and her own free-spirited personality, practically that of a prototype "hippie," helped nurture the Diana of the Dunes identity. A tragic end put a seal on it.

Gray, born in 1888 to a prominent Chicago family, was an early female graduate of the University of Chicago (enrolled at age 16) and studied abroad in Germany, where it seems she fell under the influence of an European back-to-nature movement. She returned to Chicago and worked as a secretary at an astronomy magazine in the metropolis. Later legends would claim a broken love affair sent her into self-exile in the Indiana dunes, or possibly an argument with her family. She told one reporter that failing eyesight made her lose her job, another that working was "slavery," and she relocated to the Indiana shoreline, east of Gary, in 1915 because she was familiar with the area from childhood excursions, scientific dissertations, and articles she had written.

She turned an abandoned fisherman's hovel into a home. There she hunted ducks for food, walked seven miles to the town of Porter for provisions and library books, sold game and berries to visitors, and generally lived off the land and her past earnings. Allegedly the first "Diana of the Dunes" article came about via the jealous wife of a fisherman. The man had seen a mysterious newcomer skinny-dipping and his spouse complained to the newspapers.

Nonetheless, Alice Gray was rather dowdy, weathered, and middle-aged — not the moonlit nymph the Hearst press would make of her — and something of a feminist and conservationist in her opinions. Though she had a reputation of chasing off unwanted intruders with her guns, Gray was not publicity-shy. In 1917, during a "Great Dunes Pageant," the celebrated Diana of the Dunes took to the speaker podium to talk about the importance of preserving the Indiana dunes as a park. She published articles arguing her case and was attacked in editorial pages by opinion-leaders who wanted the dunes area cleared for heavy-industry factories.

Even though her solitude helped feed the legend, Gray did not, in fact, live entirely alone. She is said to have had at least two children, possibly by different fathers, though details are vague about the first ("an Indian," according to one account). Around 1920 or so Alice Gray took up with a carpenter who used the name Paul Wilson (according to later reporters an alias for Paul Eisenblatter, a convict), an imposing six-footer. They moved to a cottage called Wren's Nest at the western end of Ogden Dunes. Stories of their relationship here diverge, based on the sentiment of the teller.

It seems unlikely indeed that such an independent woman was a battered spouse, but there are reports to that effect. Other narratives claim they were truly in love, but trouble followed 'Paul Wilson' like a cloud, and he was accused of theft from neighboring residences and the mutilation-murder of a man whose corpse was found on the beach. Alice suffered a skull injury from which she never quite recovered. Most accounts blame that wound not on Paul, but a deputy sheriff/self-styled security guard, who tangled with the couple.

With the area being developed for homes, Alice and Paul attempted to move to Texas, but returned to the Indiana dunes. Alice M. Gray died at home on February 11, 1925. The initial verdict was uremic poisoning, but one later author claimed the autopsy also showed internal damage to the abdomen, symptomatic of beatings. At her memorial service, Paul — in jail at the time of her passing — brandished a gun at mourners and reporters and was arrested. Some sources say nobody knows what became of him (or their two children); others say Paul married another woman a year later, continued a criminal career, and was either shot during a caper or died in prison.

In a final lash of fate, Alice Gray's interment was handled by a crooked sexton who buried the dead atop one another to save space. Thus her actual gravesite in Oak Lawn Cemetery in Gary is not certain. Her memory persists, however, in both Hoosier folklore and the legend of a nude woman running along the sand or disappearing into the water. Her beloved dunes were indeed made into a state park in 1923 and then a national one in 1966.

Author and former National Park Service ranger Andrea Lankford sought to confirm sightings of Alice's phantom among the staff of the Indiana Dunes National Lakeshore, but could only hear second- and third-hand rumors that a ranger had spotted the ghost in 1972. Regional festivals and a "Diana of the Dunes" beauty pageant have kept her name alive locally, and, while the vague ghost reports may be further embellishment of the facts, it seems fitting that mythology ultimately enfold the woman nicknamed after a Roman goddess… *Diana, She Who Hunts Alone.*

DOC (See *DANIEL J. MORRELL*)

DOOR OF DEATH (See PORTE DES MORTES)

DREAMER'S ROCK (See MANITOULIN ISLAND)

DUNNING, CAPTAIN GEORGE (See LAKE MICHIGAN TRIANGLE)

DURAND EASTMAN PARK — A park in Monroe County, part of Rochester, New York, bordering Lake Ontario, is the site of a regional GHOST folktale said to have taken place in the nineteenth century. The teenage daughter of a local woman (whose name is sometimes given as Elise) who lived near the beach disappeared after one of her daily strolls along the shore. The girl had earlier told her mother she had an ominous feeling about a male neighbor. The grieving mother told police the man was doubtlessly guilty, of kidnapping, rape, and murder, but she could prove none of her suspicions, and spent days searching the marshes for her child's body, accompanied by her dogs. Finally, in desperation, the mother committed suicide by throwing herself off a cliff into the waters of Lake Ontario. Not long afterwards her dogs died of heartbreak.

In death, the mother returned as an *apparition* known as the White Lady. Once again joined by her faithful hounds, she still patrols the present-day Durand Eastman Park, especially on foggy autumn nights. Some stories describe her as emerging specifically from Durand Lake in the park. Further embroidery on the tale states that a parapet-like brick structure overlooking the lake is the White Lady's "castle" (it was actually built for Civil Defense purposes) and that her husband had been an abusive spouse whom she killed in self-defense, only to lose her precious daughter to similar violence. Therefore White Lady (alternatively known as the Lady in White) is openly hostile to men, harassing them (and their vehicles), trying to chase them from the park. She will not torment women, however. In fact, a fetching corollary to the legend is that if a woman suspects her man of infidelity, she should bring him to Durand Eastman Park's equivalent of Lovers Lane. Then the White Lady will materialize — visible only to the man — and he will have no choice but to confess any indiscretions.

In 2001 a local "paranormal investigator" publicized a grainy and indistinct image as the first photograph of the White Lady. Meanwhile, local skeptics have declared that area police archives record no such murder, suicide, or missing-persons case in the files. The resemblance to the Hispanic mythology of LA LLORONA is striking and perhaps significant.

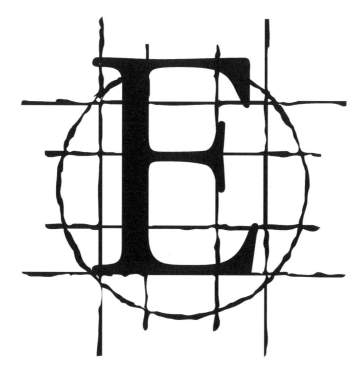

EAGLE HARBOR LIGHTHOUSE — Built in 1871 at Eagle Harbor, Michigan, this lighthouse overlooks Lake Superior. The Norman Gothic style building replaced an earlier lighthouse dating back to the early 1850s, and in 1912 a lifesaving station was built nearby. During World War II, the Eagle Harbor Lighthouse and grounds became a Coast Guard training facility, and Coast Guardsmen reports as well as rumors have perpetuated GHOST stories about both the brick lighthouse and the keepers' house (a second keeper's house, meanwhile, is said to be notably ghost-free). Phenomena from the lighthouse building itself include sounds of furniture being moved, heavy footfalls, and ceiling lights switched on and off mysteriously. One Coast Guardsman, flustered with the inexplicable sounds and sights, moved into the first keeper's house—only to find it equally bewitched, especially with resonant, traveling footsteps. He finally found relief by relocating to the other house. An unnamed witness claimed to have gotten an unnerving sighting of the ghost—a faceless man in a flannel shirt—in the lighthouse bedroom late one night. At least one of the lighthouse keepers, Stephen Cocking, died while at the lighthouse back in 1889. In the 1980s Eagle Harbor Lighthouse became a maritime museum operated by the Keweenaw County Historical Society.

EMILY (See SHIP NAMES)

EASTLAND **DISASTER** — One the worst maritime disasters in US history occurred with the partial capsizing of this pleasure ship in Chicago in twenty-one feet of water on a calm summer day in 1915. The wake of the tragedy left a legacy of local GHOST stories and anecdotes of OMENS and PROPHECIES, including screams and momentous splashing heard at the accident site both before and weeks after the terrible event.

The *Eastland* was a packet steamer constructed by Jenks Shipbuilding Company, under a commission from the Michigan Steamship Company, and launched in 1903 on the Black River of Port Huron, Michigan. The only passenger boat Jenks ever completed, she was designed to serve as a speedy and luxurious excursion boat on the Great Lakes. She had oak paneling and mahogany parlors, two levels of observation decks, numerous staterooms, a saloon, and steam calliope, and a capacity of 3,300 passengers and seventy crewmembers. This figure would become vitally important later.

In her first year of service, the vessel displayed a tendency to rock as much as thirty to forty degrees to starboard, and modifications were duly made and her official human capacity reduced to 2,800, then upgraded to 2,907, and then down to 2,400...as the ship continued to have close calls with floundering and owners measured the safety risks against their drive to sell as many tickets as possible. In 1909, a consortium of investors purchased the boat and answered the charges against the *Eastland* with an ad in a Cleveland newspaper offering $5,000 to anyone who could prove beyond a doubt she was unsound. They claimed the rumors were a slander campaign begun by rival pleasure-boat operators. Nonetheless, in 1913, a naval architect wrote to the harbormaster of Port of Chicago that the *Eastland* suffered innate structural defects and had shown instability and a tendency to list to one side during routine inspections.

There still appears to be some opinion that even a perfectly good vessel might not have borne the burden placed on the *Eastland* early on Saturday, July 24, 1915, when she was to convey a full load of merrymakers from Chicago to a popular annual picnic among the sand dunes of Michigan City, Indiana. More than 7,300 tickets had been sold for the trip (those not taking the *Eastland* could avail themselves of a second steamer, the *Theodore Roosevelt*), most of them immigrants who were employees and family members connected with Western Electric Company. Later it would be proposed that the seventy-five-cent tickets were so aggressively peddled to the company's employees that many of the victims felt they had no choice but to go, lest they lose their jobs (something the company strongly denied).

Foretastes of disaster included a newlywed husband and wife, the Jahnkes, who suffered disturbing dreams before the trip and left jewelry and money behind for their relatives...in the event they did not return. Another Western Electric employee—a teenager described as an amateur fortuneteller—confided to her mother a dread of going, but was persuaded to embark and indeed...she never came back alive. A Chicago resident claimed a friend visiting from Texas experienced a vision in the hallway of the Palmer House of a giant ship on its side and row upon row of corpses.

When the *Eastland* pulled away from the pier on the Chicago River that morning, her decks were packed with about 3,500 people. Straightaway she began an awful lean to port, then starboard. There is an assertion, disputable, that the impending disaster was aggravated when passengers rushed to one side of the vessel to have their picture taken by a photographer prominently set up on the opposite bank of the river. Attempts by the crew to compensate with the ship's ballast tanks were unsuccessful. As a ragtime band played, the ship began a steep, final lean to port, half overturning in the river at approximately 7:20 a.m. Cruelly, the lifejackets were stowed away in locked wooden containers over the passenger compartments. That design flaw, along with the lifeboats held aloft, had made the ship further top-heavy.

Even though rescuers were on the scene in an instant to pull survivors from the river, the tragedies of those trapped in the submerged end of the ship multiplied—more than enough to keep headline-writers busy as the scale of the calamity unfolded.

- A teenage Western Electric employee, just chosen beauty queen of the plant, died in one of the cabins.
- A fireman involved in rescue efforts discovered the sodden corpse of his own little daughter among the dead.
- The *Eastland*'s captain, Harry Pedersen, possibly dazed from a blow to the head as the ship turned over, quarreled and interfered with lifesavers as they started cutting into the hull with acetylene torches.

Bodies of the 844 dead recovered—some sources say 852—were all conveyed to makeshift morgues, filling the 2nd Regiment Armory Building on Washington Street; numbered and lain on the floor in rows of eighty-five...much as the visitor from Texas had foreseen. There exists a news photograph of a stunned fireman cradling the body of a drowned boy from the *Eastland*; in both impact and composition, it is remarkably similar to press images from eighty years later—of a fireman holding a dead child after the Oklahoma City bombing. For the city of Chicago (and Cicero, where many of the Western Electric employees lived), the *Eastland* was no less a trauma. Mass funerals took place the following Wednesday, and the inquest and trial to determine who was at fault turned into a decades-long legal wrangle that ultimately, in 1935, declared the *Eastland* had indeed been seaworthy, all but perhaps her ballast tanks. Pedersen maintained that the *Eastland* had stumbled on an uncharted obstruction on the river bottom, causing her accident. He never commanded a ship again. Chief engineer, Joseph Erickson, cited by some historians as a hero for shutting down the boilers inside the half-sunken wreck to prevent an explosion and worse horror, died at age thirty-seven in 1919 of heart disease; he would later be singled out by the courts as being at fault, perhaps a convenient scapegoat.

Indeed, despite intense media coverage and editorial page finger-pointing, there were no monuments or lasting memorials to the many victims, except for the permanent cancellation of that annual picnic. With America's entry into World War I, the *Eastland*'s hulk was refurbished by the US Navy as a home-front gunship renamed the *Wilmette*. With no attention to her dark history, she carried FDR and his cabinet, and welcomed visitors as a showcase military vessel on the Great Lakes. She was cut up for scrap in 1947.

The ghost stories associated with the *Eastland* center on the old armory on Washington and Curtis Streets in Chicago, which, in 1915, served as a temporary morgue for so many dead that wicker baskets and other ersatz containers were used for coffins. When the National Guard established a new armory elsewhere, the old building became, by turns, a Post Office vehicle depot, a horse stable, a bowling alley, and a film and TV studio. In recent years, the site has become part of Harpo Studios, headquarters for the popular TV talk show hosted by Oprah Winfrey. Tales of the paranormal began to circulate in 1989, shortly after Harpo Studios opened. Workers on the night shift speak of doors opening and closing of their own volition and the unaccountable odor of lilac perfume. A "Gray Lady" apparition, dressed in early 1900s fashion, has been said to wander the halls and even shows up on security cameras. A guard has spoken of hearing sobbing, crashing sounds, and laughter—once so severe that a terrified producer locked herself in her office.

Another building where the dead were housed had employees afraid to venture into the basement and the third floor, said to be haunted by a mischievous child ghost. There are even stories that apparitions of bodies of *Eastland's* drowning victims continue to be seen bobbing in the Chicago River, almost a century later. Another Chicago-area ghost, the macabre SEAWEED CHARLIE, is also sometimes associated with the *Eastland*.

Not until June 9, 1989, was a plaque unveiled at the edge of the city's river honoring the fatalities of the *Eastland* disaster.

EDMUND FITZGERALD — At the time of this writing, this was the "youngest" Great Lakes GHOST SHIP. Her tragic sinking in November 1975, on a stormy Lake Superior, is a living-memory maritime tragedy, commemorated in popular song and yearly observance, and a number of paranormal rumors and innuendo have become attached to the loss of the vessel and all twenty-nine men aboard her.

The first lake boat to be built of prefabricated steel sub-assemblies, the 729-foot, 8,686-ton freighter was launched in 1958. She had been named for a prominent Milwaukee banker, and at the christening ceremony, it took Mrs. Edmund Fitzgerald three tries before the champagne bottle finally broke on her hull. According to maritime SUPERSTITION, this foretold bad luck, though in no way was the early career of the 'Fitz' darkened by the omen. She was a state-of-the-art ore freighter, equipped with all the modern conveniences, two plush passenger staterooms, and lifesaving gear. Dubbed by some "Queen of the Lakes" (by others, probably because of the name, "King of the Lakes"), the *Edmund Fitzgerald* served as a proud flagship of the Columbia Transportation Company. Only in death did she become synonymous with disaster.

She embarked on a final run of the season November 9, 1975. The great ship, under veteran Captain Ernest McSorley, had taken on a load of palletized ore at Superior, Wisconsin, intended for the blast furnaces of Detroit (subsequent rumors claimed she was overloaded, but an inquest determined this was not so). A fierce gale and snowstorm blew up, prompting Coast Guard warnings that all vessels on Lake Superior, no matter what size, seek shelter. On the night of November 10th Captain McSorley made last radio contact with the freighter *Arthur Anderson*. Captain Jesse Cooper, of the *Arthur Anderson*, had been talking to the *Fitzgerald's* captain just moments before the great ship disappeared. Cooper stated the ore carrier was in a heavy snow squall and could barely be seen. When the snow ended, the *Edmund Fitzgerald* had vanished...not only from sight, but from Cooper's radar as well.

That was the end of the ship, with no distress signals—despite state-of-the-art radio equipment—only minimal wreckage, and no bodies recovered. Later some rendered the judgment she had been torn apart by the mysterious Lake Superior wave phenomenon THE THREE SISTERS. It was also theorized that the ship had bottomed out on a very dangerous and then-unknown rock formation, called Caribou Shoal, and began filling with water and sinking before the crew had time to react, or even send a radio distress signal. The absence of survivors ensured that what ultimately happened to the ship and her men would become a source of speculation forevermore.

The *Edmund Fitzgerald's* hull was found in 530 feet of water in August 1977. At that depth, exploration was limited to submersibles and further expeditions revealed that the ship was broken in two pieces; one hull section gapingly gashed. But had that sundering happened on the surface, as with the *DANIEL J. MORRELL* (from which one lone survivor was able to give investigators a full account), or after the fatal accident and sinking? Different investigators have argued most strenuously over whether a freak accident or poor maintenance and mental fatigue doomed the ship in a manner so rapidly that nobody even had time to transmit a final SOS.

Doubtless much of the paranormal fame of the "Mighty Fitz," can be traced to an eerie popular song by Canadian balladeer Gordon Lightfoot, "The Wreck of the *Edmund Fitzgerald*," which as a refrain cites INDIAN LEGENDS:

"The lake so it's said
Never gives up her dead
When the gales of November come early."

Duluth resident Wendy Mitchell reported that she and her boyfriend had seen the unmistakable freighter on Halloween night, in 1980, entering Duluth's harbor and passing under the Aerial Bridge, which, accommodatingly, raised to admit the great ship.

Mitchell said her boyfriend talked to bridge operators, who said they were were duly signaled by the "ghost" and could hear the sounds of sledgehammers opening hatches as the ship passed beneath.

Some comment has been made in the UFOS and USOS counterculture of a sinister connection between a spate of UFO reports over the Great Lakes at the very time the *Edmund Fitzgerald* went down. The absence of crew bodies, a detail seized upon by "alien-abduction" theorists, appears to have ended in 1994, when one of a succession of mini-submarine dives to the wreck disclosed decomposing human remains, clad in a canvas lifejacket, on the lake bottom. (It is remotely possible that this particular corpse was a victim from some other calamity and not a *Fitzgerald* hand, however.) While other Great Lakes sinkings took a greater toll in lives, the loss of the "Fitz" still caused public grief into the twenty-first century—and a generation knows it as the "worst disaster in Great Lakes history" and, hence, a font of modern myth-making. (See also SPLIT ROCK LIGHTHOUSE)

ELLA ELLENWOOD — This lumber-hauling schooner, built in 1870, has become a Lake Michigan GHOST SHIP by obscure local reputation. The 157-ton, 106-foot sailing vessel reportedly reappeared despite battered to pieces in a 1901 gale north of Milwaukee, at Fox Point. In a noteworthy exception to many legends of phantom boats, the crew of the *Ella Ellenwood* did not die with her, but escaped safely to shore. The phantom is said to reappear just off White Lake, Michigan, her longtime homeport, which lies more or less directly across the lake's expanse opposite Fox Point.

EMPEROR — A 525-foot long steel ore freighter built in 1910 by the Collingwood Shipbuilding Company of Ontario, she served for thirty-seven years on the Great Lakes until June 4, 1947...when, with 10,000 tons of bulk iron ore, she ran aground on Canoe Rocks, near ISLE ROYALE, and effectively broke in two. The force of the suction as she went under sank one of the life rafts into the chilled water, accounting for most of the dozen crewmembers being killed, including the captain and first mate. Great Lakes historian Frederick Stonehouse collected a tale from a scuba diver who logged a rare underwater ghost sighting on board the sunken *Emperor*. In one of the deckhand's cabins, the aquanaut saw a phantom sailor...peacefully reclining in a bunk bed, *looking back at him*. The diver made a hasty retreat, writes Stonehouse.

ERIE BABY — Also known as "Baby Erie," this footnote in the lore of SOUTH BAY BESSIE was initially displayed as a three-foot-long, dragon-like creature, stuffed, and mounted by Larry Peterson, a taxidermist and bait-shop proprietor in Lakewood, Ohio, who had found the decayed, unfamiliar-looking fish with a hook through its mouth on Lake Erie's shoreline in the early 1990s. Wanting to make an impression at an upcoming trade show, Peterson followed a time-honored tradition of taxidermists who manipulate animal parts into strange and whimsical shapes. In the carnival freak-show trade, such creations are called "gaffs." In nautical lore, doctored fish (especially skates or rays sliced and posed to present a quasi-humanoid physiognomy) are called "Jenny Hanivers."

Peterson twisted the fish into a dinosaur-like pose, connoting a long neck, trimmed the dorsal fin into a series of serrations, and added pieces of skin to suggest little anterior and posterior 'flippers.' Word of the curiosity reached the proponents of "Creationism," who in the 1980s and 1990s were turning (somewhat illogically) to LAKE MONSTERS to bolster their religious claim that the *Book of Genesis* was literal and Darwin's theory of evolution untrue. Carl Baugh, of the Texas-based Creation Evidence Museum, journeyed to Lakewood by the end of the decade and actually purchased "Erie Baby" to display. The specimen was posted on Creationist websites as a possible juvenile dinosaur, potentially of the plesiosaur family — inferring the infant stage of the creature that would ultimately grow into the legendary *Lake Erie Monster*.

But any remotely scientific scrutiny would reveal that this is a composite chimera, not credible as an unknown animal. Glen J. Kuban, a Great Lakes angler and Internet blogger with an interest in such curious matters, published an opinion that Erie Baby most closely resembled a manipulated burbot, or ling-cod (species Lota Lota), an elongated, almost eel-like Great Lakes fish, capable of reaching a yard in length, unfamiliar even to most fishermen due to its preference for deep waters. This bottom-dweller is also known colloquially as the "lawyerfish."

ERIE BOARD OF TRADE — A GHOST SHIP schooner, it's the stage setting for one of the most famous—and most repeated—of all Great Lakes ghost stories. The tale of the *Erie Board of Trade* and her doom was written in shipping newspapers and verse. Yet attempts by researchers to specifically locate evidence that a ship called *Erie Board of Trade* and her captain ever existed proved futile. James Donahue, who has compiled a website of GHOST SHIP tales, says it's a deliberate fabrication. Nonetheless, it gained popular attention by appearing in colorful, novelistic detail in the *New York Sun* newspaper of August 20, 1883, and was soon reprinted as factual in several newspapers in waterfront towns around the Great Lakes.

The phantom ship is supposedly spotted in Saginaw Bay. The stories claim that a wrathful GHOST wrecked the cursed three-master, which disappeared in Lake Huron in 1883. The captain of the ship, named as Captain Jack Caster, of Milan (unspecified whether the Milan in Michigan, Ohio, or even Tennessee), had taken a dislike to a new crewmember, a Scot with a mane of red hair. He ordered the crewman to go up the main mast to the boatswain's chair, even though everyone knew that the ropes were frayed. Half-drunk and angry, the captain demanded that the Scot obey. The crewman ended up falling fatally to the deck, and with his dying breath, he cursed the ship. Soon, *his ghost* started to appear on the deck, in the cabins, and, night after night, darting amidst the riggings. Sailors who did not see the apparition personally heard of the haunting while they were in port; some of them took the ghost as an ill OMEN and refused to sign back on.

Captain Caster was hard-pressed to recruit new sailors. The ones who quit lived to tell the tale because, on her next voyage, the *Erie Board of Trade* vanished—or, in some versions, went down about fifteen miles north of Deer Park, which is located on Lake Superior. It is said that her phantom has since been seen sailing the bay. Lee Murdock, an Illinois-based singer of Great Lakes chanties and ghost stories, recorded a ballad based on the story that gives the ghost sailor the name 'Red Monroe.'

Recently Great Lakes writers such as Wes Oleszewski and Frederick Stonehouse have discovered a very similar story dating to the 1870s, but naming the schooner involved as the *Reindeer* and sinking/disappearing in Lake Ontario "on a calm summer night" somewhere off Oswego. Here the martinet captain is named Dunn and the ghost in the riggings, curiously, is female—the ship's cook, who was crushed below deck when the *Reindeer* collided with another vessel. In this version, the ship does not recur as a phantom.

ERIE L. HACKLEY (See OMENS and PROPHECIES)

ERIE WAVE (See JINXES and JONAHS)

EVENING STAR (See SHIP NAMES)

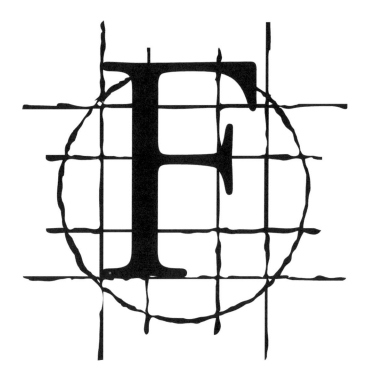

F.A. MEYER (See SUPERSTITIONS)

FAIRPORT HARBOR LIGHTHOUSE — In Fairport Harbor, Ohio, on Lake Erie, this is the popular name for the Fairport Harbor Old Main Lighthouse of 1871, made obsolete by the 1925 construction of the Fairport Harbor West Breakwater Lighthouse, which is still active. The old, conical lighthouse, rising seventy feet at the end of the town of Fairport Harbor, and its keeper's house, have since been added to the National Register of Historic Places and the Fairport Harbor Historical Society has turned it into a maritime museum. It is also the scene of a *nonstandard* GHOST story. There have been rumors that the small son of a lighthouse keeper, a boy named Robbie Babcock who died of smallpox, still lingers in spirit form, but the most famous Fairport Harbor spook is not even that of a person.

Allegedly the former curator of the museum, who lived for a time at the complex, would glimpse a cat running around the place. She owned no cat, nor did she allow strays inside, but nonetheless had an impression of a feline skittering about, to the point that she would amuse the phantom cat by making a toy out of a rolled-up

The **FAIRPORT HARBOR LIGHTHOUSE** and museum...allegedly haunted by a cat ghost.

sock, throwing it, and watching the shadowy cat chase after it. She also claimed to feel an invisible cat jump in bed with her at night.

In 2001, when workmen were installing a new ventilation system for air conditioning in a crawlspace beneath the lighthouse, one of them literally found himself face-to-face with the desiccated body of a cat, eyeless and mummified by the climate. The little carcass was recovered from its hiding place left propped up by the stairs for the museum's publicist to find. She claimed she screamed at first sight of it. Ultimately the news media had a field day with the tale, that the "source" of the ghost rumors had a tangible foundation—or at least as tangible as such things ever get.

Some writers have linked the dead cat with the Babcock family, stating that it could have been one of many pets that kept the grieving Mrs. Babcock comforted after losing Robby. One psychic researcher though, noted an arcane and esoteric practice of ritually sealing up an animal in the masonry of a building for luck and wondered if this SUPERSTITION might possibly have prevailed during the construction of the lighthouse (or an even older lighthouse that predated it) in a community largely consisting of Finns. Whether a pagan sacrifice, a lost pet, or an incidental stray, the mummified cat went on public display under glass in the museum for a time, but the macabre remains were later removed.

FEU FOLLET (See SPOOK LIGHTS)

FINNS — Finnish ship captains and officers, during the age of sail especially, were often favored in the hiring practices of Great Lakes shipping companies. Ethnic Finns maintained a collective reputation as skillful and thrifty skippers and seafarers. Resentment by the general sailor population at the disproportionate number of Finns in positions of authority blended with anti-immigrant sentiment and maritime *superstition* in some degrees, to spawn whispered rumors and folktales about the Finns. They were said to have had black-magic powers—and even struck bargains with the devil—to calm or survive dangerously storm-tossed waters. Fortunately such slander belongs to a remote past. Finnish cultural festivals and celebrations persist in shoreline communities such as Fairport Harbor on Lake Erie, where Finnish family names predominate in the town cemetery.

FORESTER CAMPGROUNDS (See QUAY HOUSE)

GARIBALDI (See SPOOK LIGHTS)

GEORGE F. WHITNEYS (See GHOST SHIPS)

GEORGE G. HADLEY (See JINXES and JONAHS)

GHOST — Tales of ghosts haunting ships, lighthouses, and coastlines are many; there may be a connection to an old SUPERSTITION that an earthbound spirit is restricted by or unable to cross running water. While orthodox science has never recognized a ghost as genuine, parapsychologists and other fringe-science investigators-authors have attempted to quantify/qualify what would otherwise be considered good old-fashioned "spooks." Traditional ghosts are taken to be spirit or entities...the restless remnants of the dead, unable to find peace in the afterlife for one reason or another. In the most famous of all Great Lakes ghost stories—*ERIE BOARD OF TRADE*—the specter is an avenging crewman, determined to hound the ship and captain who killed him to their collective doom (on the note of hounds, the origin of the BLACK DOG OF LAKE ERIE is thematically similar).

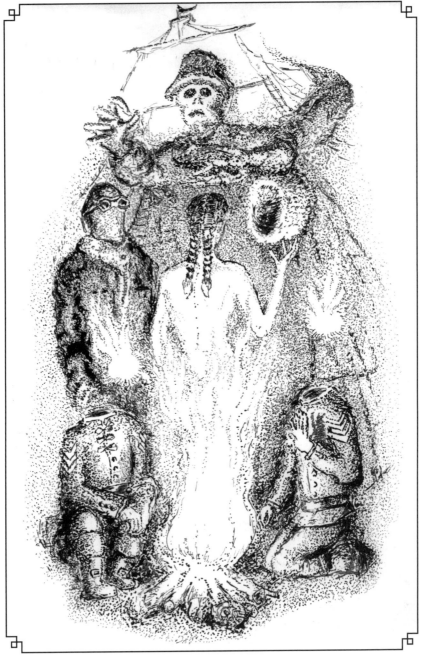

GHOSTS of the Great Lakes range from the enticing **DIANA OF THE DUNES** to headless soldiers to **SPOOK LIGHTS** to the pilot **SEAWEED CHARLIE** to a dreadful "Rolling Muff"...

However, some paranormal investigators have come to view certain apparitions as a non-sentient form of energy merely "playing back" images of the past, like a repeating movie-projector image (though by what exact mechanism or medium is unknown). GHOST SHIPS might seem a very good argument for this. In some cases ghostly manifestations occur strictly as sounds. The term "poltergeist," literally translated, means "noisy ghost," and, by some strict definitions, a poltergeist is by its very nature unseen, though visible manifestations of its actions occur in the form of flung objects and commensurate damage, mysteriously arranged furniture or clothing, or even strange writing. On the Great Lakes, however, the ghost accounts of *IRONSIDES* and the *JANE MILLER* reflect hauntings in the form of untraceable cries and voices. Other lesser-known forms of 'ghosts' include "forerunners" or "tokens," regional nicknames for a type of phantom (technically called a "crisis apparition") that appears as more or less an omen. It is seen coincident to or simultaneous with the original human's death. In paranormal tales, this type of spirit usually materializes before family members, often over very great distances.

Author and cynic Ambrose Bierce was of the opinion that all ghosts should logically be nude; otherwise clothing would have had souls, which makes an interesting commentary on the legend of Lake Michigan's *DIANA OF THE DUNES*. In many ghost accounts, it seems that an apparition is visible to some witnesses, but not others. Records from November 1901 tell of an Irish immigrant named Hugh McKenna, hired as a sailor on board the 267-foot packet steamer *Syracuse*, who either was insane or serves as an especially poignant example of this type of phenomenon. During his first—and last—trip as part of the *Syracuse* crew complement, McKenna spent much of his time apparently dazed or in conversations with an invisible companion, whom he told shipmates was his sister, who had accompanied him to Buffalo, but took ill and died, leaving him alone and grief-stricken. McKenna would repeatedly pursue the "sister" throughout the ship and try to point her out to others, who saw nothing. Ultimately McKenna was locked away, but during a storm on Lake Michigan, he somehow escaped and flung himself overboard.

It was common practice during the great age of Great Lakes shipping that when a wreck occurred, and an unmanageable quantity of bodies floated ashore, to simply bury the corpses on the beach, in sand above the waterline, with temporary markers. In theory relatives would return to claim their loved ones. Obviously, in a few cases, none did. Some storytellers have credited the hastily interred, restless dead with causing

SPOOK LIGHTS and other phenomena. Another old folk-belief claims that if an individual dies in a room with a mirror that is uncovered, the spirit remains trapped in the looking-glass and will be seen peering out; this explanation has been advanced for at least one major haunted lighthouse with a reappearing apparition in its mirror.

Ghosts in lighthouses along the Great Lakes—and indeed along all the world's seas—practically constitute a whole realm of hauntings in themselves. Storytellers suggest that the loneliness, isolation, and rigor of yesteryear's light-tending profession (and perhaps again, the presence of water) tended to foster spirits, most likely lightkeepers who felt so duty-bound that not even death prevents them from returning to their cherished lighthouse towers. There may be a more prosaic explanation, however. The various non-profit organizations and historical societies maintaining old lighthouses as museums and historic sites often require donations for the upkeep of the facilities. It is considered especially good business practice to claim a haunting, either fabricating one out of whole cloth or nurturing the existing legends. It is said that ghost rumors will endear the public to an old lighthouse and increase the visitors' generosity.

To judge from the listings here, one might well presume that every Great Lakes lighthouse purports to be haunted, but that is not quite true. Many lighthouses marked by tragedies and murder among the keepers do not necessarily uphold the standard rumors of footsteps in the disused tower or anomalous noises, though one case that shows how fixedly such rumors take hold is that of the Toledo Harbor Lighthouse. It sheltered, at least for a time, a true "working ghost." This square, brick 1904 structure stands in the shallows twelve miles out in Maumee Bay on Lake Erie. After being automated in 1966, no keeper was needed on the tiny artificial island of boulders on which the tower stood, and the Coast Guard feared that vandals might trespass at the unprotected site. In 1986, they secretly installed a department-store mannequin wearing a keeper's uniform in a second-floor window of the Toledo Harbor Lighthouse. The distant sightings of the figure by boaters inspired whispers of the "Phantom of the Lighthouse," and, whether by chance or intentionally, the Toledo Harbor Lighthouse obtained its guardian spirit.

Some ghost tales seem commemorative in nature. Like a bronze statue in a park, they pay tribute to larger-than-life characters and events that even death cannot fully extinguish them. One example may be Tom Stripe, of the ONTONAGON LIGHTHOUSE. Another might be the ill-fated freighter *EDMUND FITZGERALD*.

One famous Great Lakes ghost story specifies very little in terms of names and ships, except that it concerns a one-legged captain who worked on Lake Huron. At some point in the 1880s, during a terrible storm, he washed overboard and drowned. No body was ever recovered, but the wooden leg, identified by the captain's carved initials, floated ashore and was delivered to his widow. She mounted it above the fireplace. One night, a year later a similar terrible storm blew, and the captain's young son, awakening to strange noises, beheld the leg appearing to twitch, quiver, and shake on its own. When he told his mother, she agreed with him, that the father's ghost had come on the winds. In fact, the captain had appeared in her dreams that very night. Several days later the widow was dead — as though summoned to the next world by the captain. The son buried the wooden leg with his mother.

For serious (or non-serious) ghost watching, complete with paid tours, the most haunted place by reputation, on the Great Lakes would probably be the Canadian community of Niagara-on-the-Lake (formerly Newark) in Ontario. Another prime contender would be MACKINAC ISLAND.

(See also: AU SABLE, BIG BAY POINT LIGHTHOUSE, BIG MCCOY ISLAND, BLUE BANKS, CHARLES POINT, COVE ISLAND LIGHT, DURAND EASTMAN PARK, *EASTLAND* DISASTER, FAIRPORT HARBOR LIGHTHOUSE, GIBRALTER POINT LIGHTHOUSE, *IRONSIDES*, GRAND ISLAND NORTH LIGHT, ISLE ROYALE, JOHNSONS ISLAND, KARSTEN INN, KELLEYS ISLAND, LA LLORONA, *LAFAYETTE*, LONG POINT, MANITOU ISLANDS, MANITOULIN ISLAND, *NAHANT*, OSWEGO BREAKWATER LIGHTHOUSE, PIPE ISLAND LIGHTHOUSE, POINT AUX BARQUES, PRESQUE ISLE NEW LIGHTHOUSE, PRESQUE ISLE OLD LIGHTHOUSE, QUAY HOUSE, RASPBERRY ISLAND LIGHTHOUSE, *ROGER BLOUGH*, SEAWEED CHARLIE, SEBASTIAN, SEUL CHOIX LIGHTHOUSE, SOUTH BASS ISLAND LIGHTHOUSE, SPLIT ROCK LIGHTHOUSE, ST. MARTIN ISLAND LIGHTHOUSE, STANNARD ROCK LIGHTHOUSE, *STE. CLAIRE*, *SUCCESS*, TALBOT ISLAND, THREE-FINGERED REILLY, THUNDER BAY ISLAND, WAUGOSHANCE SHOAL LIGHTHOUSE, WHITE RIVER LIGHT STATION, and YEO ISLAND)

GHOST SHIPS — While folklore has preserved tales of ghost trains, and even (on rare occasion) cars, the inanimate object most often reported is the classic "ghost ship." Seafarers will say it's proof that a ship has a soul...a *spirit* that survives beyond death/destruction/sinking. That is why one must always use the personal pronoun "she" for a ship—not "it"—and this book respectfully complies. (Why ships are female is an entirely separate SUPERSTITION.) One should note a rather confusing taxonomy, that, in regional parlance, "ghost ship" need not refer to a craft that seems to rise from a watery grave and

Lake Superior Ghost Ships:

• The *Cerisoles* and the *Inkerman*: two minesweepers built at the Port William shipyards in Canada intended for service in the First World War, but vanished on the lake in 1918 instead.

• The *Clemson*, lost with all hands in 1908 with only (maybe) one hatch cover found (a wreck investigated in 2007 was thought to be the *Clemson*, but turned out to be the Cyrus instead).

• The barge *Comrade*, being towed by a steamer, vanished in a Lake Superior gale in September 1890 after the rope snapped.

Lake Michigan Ghost Ships:

Many Michigan "ghost ships" have been retroactively classified as victims of the LAKE MICHIGAN TRIANGLE, including the schooner *George F. Whitney*, gone with all hands in 1872, in a case called "peculiar" in the annals because, in advance of the disappearance, the captain adopted a habit of flying all ship flags at half-mast. (He claimed it was his unorthodox way of signaling tug boats.)

Lake Erie Ghost Ships:

• The two-year-old schooner *South American* vanished in 1843.

• The schooner *Kate Norton* gone—without a clue—in 1863.

• *Radiant*, *Maumee Valley*, *Jersey City*, *Dacotah*, and the tug *Silver Spray*.

Lake Ontario Ghost Ships:

• The tug *Frank E. Barnes* vanished in the so-called MARYSBURGH VORTEX in 1915.

Lake Huron Ghost Ships:

• The great whaleback *Clifton*; this classic ghost ship vanished in stormy weather on September 22, 1924 with a crew of twenty-eight. It still hasn't been found, even by modern divers, though immediate searches turned up bits of the pilothouse.

• Only a few oars, uniforms, and odds and ends were found after the Georgian Bay steamer *Jane Miller* vanished in November 1881.

• A lone yawl was the only remainder of the schooner *Kate L. Bruce*, lost in a November 8, 1887 storm.

• Other ghost ships include the *Celtic* and the steamer *Eclipse*.

comport anew. The nickname is also applied to any unfortunate vessel that just sinks or disappears with no survivors and is never pinpointed again by salvagers or divers. Bad weather is almost inevitably a factor and the definition allows minor wreckage. But when a vessel of many tons, laden with cargo and crew, fails to make port ever again, without acres of flotsam, jetsam, and bodies, the mariner's phrase "*she sailed into a crack in the lake and just disappeared*" is an oft-applied vernacular.

Of "literal" ghost ships—the ships that are sighted after having been lost—some writers differentiate between two varieties: spectral ships and phantom ships.

A *spectral ship* seems to radiate with its own luminescence, to the point that the entire vessel may appear to be on fire. Spectral ships, or "fire ships," would appear more commonly on the ocean than inland lakes, like the nameless schooner that travels at impossibly high speed, seemingly ablaze, off the Lot Seven Shore of Canada's Prince Edward Island in the Atlantic, or the fabled "Palatine Light," said to be the burning refugee vessel *Prince Augusta* off Block Island, Rhode Island. The nameless specter purported to illuminate off Manitoulin Island is the Great Lakes' most prominent spectral ship.

A *phantom ship* is one that does not glow, appearing either solid or translucent. A classic and oft-retold phantom ship sighting was registered by the Canadian artist/historian Rowley Murphy in August 1910 during a pleasure cruise on an "amazingly beautiful night" on western Lake Ontario. Along with his father, a cousin, and two other yachts filled with witnesses, Murphy awakened at 1:30 a.m. and heard repeated whistle-alarm blasts from an unidentified steamer. By the moonlight he could see a smallish steamship of slightly older design, about a half-mile off shore, by the mouth of Etobikoke Creek. Its distress sirens continued sounding, so the men set out to aid the possibly stricken ship.

"As the boys in the dinghy reached the area where something definite should have been seen, there was nothing there beyond the clear and powerful moonlight, a few gulls wakened from sleep...but something else impossible to ignore. This was a succession of long, curving ripples in a more or less circular pattern, which just might have been the last appearance of those caused by the foundering of a steamer many years before, on a night of similar beauty...Something that had occurred in the more or less distant past, and which had turned to the consciences of living men after a long absence."

A photo-illustration conception of history's most famous GHOST SHIP, the *Flying Dutchman*.

No name was ever put to Murphy's vanishing ghost ship. Also unidentified was an old-fashioned steamship sighted on at least two occasions—one as recent as 1977—working her way up Minnesota's Lester River, Duluth's ship channel into Lake Superior. Local writer Hugh Bishop notes that in the same area lies the recently-discovered wreck of the *Benjamin Noble*, a 1,481-ton steel steamer, said to be grossly overloaded with cargo when she was lost with all twenty hands in the harbor in a storm one April night in 1914; she may well fit the witness descriptions, but the association is highly speculative.

(See also *ADMIRAL, ALTADOC, BANNOCKBURN, EDMUND FITZGERALD, ELLA ELLENWOOD*, GRAY GHOST, *GRIFFIN, HAMILTON* and *SCOURGE, HUDSON, HUNTER SAVIDGE, KALIYUGA, KEYSTONE STATE, LAMBTON, JOSEPH A. HOLLON, MARQUETTE & BESSEMER NO. 2*, MICHIPICOTEN ISLAND, *ONTARIO*, PORTE DES MORTES, *ST. ALBINS*, and SUNKEN SISTERS)

GHOST TOWNS — Abandoned settlements, the result of tapped-out mining or logging industries, can be found in parts of the Great Lakes. With a number of these lonely, empty (or near-empty) villages come GHOST stories.

Au Sable, near present-day Oscoda, Michigan, on Lake Huron, is the remains of the region's oldest settlement. It burned down in

1911 and many believe it to be a very haunted spot, drawing local witchcraft practitioners and other curiosity seekers. The most oft-repeated ghost story about Au Sable is that an area farm girl named Leona was accidentally shot to death by a deer hunter in 1929. Now, most often seen by deer hunters, she reappears, dressed in a winter coat and mittens. With admirable forgiveness, she is said to have found a lost deer hunter in the forest in 1979, told him she knew the woods well, and successfully led him to safety...*dematerializing* when he reached the road. Only when the hunter told his tale to a local bartender did he learn that his helpful guide was long dead.

Quite a literal "ghost town" concept has been reported by Canadian writer Michael Columbo in the aftermath of the 1957-1958 widening of the St. Lawrence River, which created the St. Lawrence Seaway and enabled international maritime traffic greater access into the Great Lakes. This was a mighty engineering project, the largest in North American history. The broadening of the waterway as well as ancillary hydroelectric dam works meant the flooding of 18,000 acres on the American side and 20,000 acres on the Canadian side, representing ten villages, eighteen cemeteries, and 8,000 homes. The vast majority of the residents went peacefully; their homes, even gardens, uprooted from their foundations and moved further inland. One Canadian Indian community resisted with six lone holdouts, but was finally persuaded to move on with bonus payments for their land. Author Jay Ehle records that they hardly had time to load up their carts when the bulldozers moved in. Ultimately the towns on the Canadian side that disappeared under the water included Aultsville, Dickinson's Landing, Farran's Point, Milles Roche, Iroquois, Morrisburg, and Moullinette. Later, according to Columbo, when ships passed over the sites of these lost villages, "murmurs" could be heard from the water, and lights — like those of a town — glimmered under the waves. (See also SHELDRAKE)

GIANT'S TOMB ISLAND (See ROCKMAN)

GIBRALTER POINT LIGHTHOUSE — It would be fitting that one of the oldest lighthouses on the Great Lakes also had a GHOST to go with it. The Gibralter Point Lighthouse was erected, overlooking Lake Ontario, on Toronto Island in 1808; only the second such Great Lakes beacon built (the first was at Niagara-on-the-Lake four years earlier). The ghost stories center on its first lighthouse keeper, John Paul Rademuller, who lived in a cabin (now vanished) next to the tower. It is said that on January 2, 1815, he was attacked by guards from nearby

Fort York, who coveted his bootleg whiskey. They chased Rademuller up the spiral stairs of the lighthouse tower to the summit, knocked him senseless, and then threw him over the edge to his death. As a grisly epilogue, the soldiers sought to cover up their crime by dismembering the body and burying the pieces in different places.

A later keeper, Joe Durnan, discovered bones—thought to be Rademuller's—in 1893. Durnan said he could hear moans and see Rademuller's ghost seeking his scattered mortal remains on foggy nights. Others say his ghost still ascended and descended the staircase to tend the beacon. In any case, however, the beacon is no longer active. Gibralter Point Lighthouse is the oldest Canadian landmark still standing on the original site and is now maintained by the Metro Toronto Parks Department, although the fifty-two-foot tower is not open to the public.

GODDESS OF BELLE ISLE (See BELLE ISLE)

GRAND ISLAND NORTH LIGHT — Grand Island is the largest island off Lake Superior's southern shore, now largely parkland. It is a destination for tourists, hikers, and bicyclists. In the INDIAN LEGENDS of the Ojibway, it was formed from the body of a giant that the Great Spirit Gitchee Manitou cast into the lake. (The Great Spirit made several such giants, but was apprehensive about actually breathing life into them; the others he left on the land to become hills around Munising, Michigan). The island is eight miles long and three miles wide, and two nearby smaller islets were considered by the Indians to be the hands of the giant. A wooden lighthouse was built on the lonely cliff on the north side of the island in 1856. Ten years later, after an official inspection, the structure was deemed in such lamentable condition that a new lighthouse was built out of sturdier brick with a squared-off forty-foot tower. A GHOST story about this lighthouse concerns a well-documented mystery.

The year was 1908. George Genry was the keeper and Edward Morrison was his assistant; they spent much of the year tending the light alone during the season. Morrison evidently confided to his wife that Genry was a difficult personality who seldom kept an assistant for more than one year. In May the two picked up provisions for the summer in Munising. That was the last anyone ever saw of George Genry. The body of Edward Morrison was found in the sailboat the two used, the vessel marooned at Au Sable. A sheriff's posse found the Grand Island North Lighthouse untended, no new logbook entries, the fresh supplies unloaded but not unpacked. Suspicion fell on Genry; thought to have killed Morrison, setting his body adrift, and then fleeing. A short time later a keeper of a lighthouse on Grand Island's southern shore claimed to have found Genry's remains on the beach, but nobody else saw this evidence. Rumors and gossip countered that George Genry had been spotted drinking in a Munising bar. His sailboat was indeed located in a dock in that town, but that was also where his family happened to live. The family themselves are credited as authors of a conspiracy theory implicating none other than William G. Mather, the president of the Cleveland Cliffs mining company and the owner of Grand Island. Allegedly the tycoon took offense at Genry and Morrison routinely poaching and hired some roughnecks to ambush and dispose of the two. But the case is considered unsolved.

The Grand Island North Lighthouse was automated in 1927, dispensing with the need for another keeper. Later the decommissioned lighthouse became a private home. George Genry's ghost has been said to persist, but the whispers have more of a folklore quality and a spooky cap to a genuine enigma of Lake Superior. The vengeful-irascible George is blamed when misfortune strikes, usually in the form of malfunctioning gear. (See also: *WILLIAM G. MATHER*)

GRAY, ALICE MABLE (See DIANA OF THE DUNES)

GRAY GHOST — Rather colorful stories from the Lake Erie Islands describe this GHOST SHIP as a "rum-runner;" one of a pesky fleet of fast vessels, powerboats outfitted with aircraft engines, that illegally sped alcohol from the Canadian side of Lake Erie to the American shores during the years of Prohibition in the 1920s and early 1930s. According to one source the Gray Ghost was actually a ship registered as *Ruby*, the captain's wife's name, but one that did business under the unofficial name *Blacksnake*. Under any name the powerboat disappeared late in 1926 while running a cache of whiskey between Pele and Kelleys Islands, possibly going down in a storm while trying to elude the US Coast Guard. But the "Gray Ghost" was reportedly seen later, still breaching over the pounding waves, the dead crew hurrying to bring an intoxicating cargo to Ohio. She may be seen scudding past in the dead of night on Erie—and if you are lucky enough to glimpse her, it is customary to raise a glass in toast.

Rumrunners, of course, were not limited to one lake. From the Les Chenaux Islands of Lake Huron comes a regional yarn that during Prohibition a sheriff—in a speedboat confiscated from a previous smuggler—pursued a Chris-Craft ferrying alcohol to the

American side. This was a rather shady lawman, according to fine details of the tale; he was especially furious that the rumrunners had refused to pay him his accustomed bribe for safe passage. Opening fire on his quarry with a .30 caliber Browning automatic rifle, the sheriff managed to hit something inflammable. The Chris-Craft exploded in a fireball, leaving no survivors. For years afterwards, on the anniversary of the tragedy, a bright flash could be seen on the water where the incident occurred, though in more recent decades the phenomena is said to occur less regularly.

GREEN MANTLE (See KAKBEKA FALLS)

GRIFFIN — Oldest of the Great Lakes GHOST SHIPS—at least the oldest one to which a name (variously spelled *Griffon*) can be placed—this sixty-foot, single-sailed, forty-five-ton barque was built of white oak in 1679 near Cayuga Creek on Lake Erie near Niagara Falls as a supply vessel. In the style of a small man-o-war, she carried small cannon and muskets as well. Her construction by shipbuilder Moyse Hillaret was supervised by pioneering French-colonial explorer Rene Robert Cavalier Sieur de La Salle, for navigating the waterways in the early days of fur trading. Her impressively carved lion-headed and eagle-winged prow was an unmistakable and unique profile on the lakes. Her maiden voyage occurred August 7th of that year. Some accounts claim the ship was cursed during construction by Metiomek, a prophet of the Iroqois tribe, converted to Christianity by the Jesuits.

On September 18 the ship, laden with pelts, disappeared on the return route from Green Bay, Wisconsin, to Fort Niagara in western New York. La Salle's chief pilot was Luc Dane, said to be a literal giant of a man. He, along with thirty crewmen, sailed into limbo with the ship, although some later rumors reached the French of an impressively tall white man being held captive by native tribes far inland, to the west. One story is that while sheltering from a storm on the Lake Michigan shore, Dane had ignored warnings by Indians to seek shelter and defiantly sailed into rough seas. A curious account from MANITOULIN ISLAND says that in the late 1800s a resident lighthouse keeper found several skeletons—one of giant stature—in a local cave, along with gold, artifacts, and coins suggesting French origin and supporting theories that some sort of mutiny or desertion (perhaps during an Indian attack) might have esued. The relics and bones kept as souvenirs by the keeper and his friends ultimately were lost.

When the *GRIFFIN* sailed on her last voyage, she went accompanied by the beat of the **OTTAWA DRUM…**

The phantom of the *Griffin* was later reported by Indian tribes dwelling along Lakes Erie, Huron, and Michigan. Sailors in the north of Lake Michigan are said to have sighted—and tried to approach—the vessel...whereupon she *dematerializes*. Lake Solitude, near Oscoda, Michigan, just north of Saginaw Bay is connected to Lake Huron by a narrow creek. A local legend states that a navigable passage once existed, but closed by supernatural means due to the sinking of the *Griffin* in this vicinity, and the restless ghosts of the crew haunt the nearby shores. (See also OTTAWA DRUM)

GROSSE ILE — An island township in the Detroit River, the largest of the Detroit River islands, and now home to a small airport and a residential population nearing a thousand, it's also the site of one of the more bizarre GHOST stories of the Great Lakes, dating back to the 1700s French settlement of the Detroit area. The story goes that in those early days, a colonist embroiled in an adulterous affair lured his unwanted wife to the swamps of Grosse Ile and murdered her, sinking her body in the mud. But he failed to account for the large, European-style hand-warming muff that she wore, which fell off in the struggle. When he went back to the marshes to retrieve the potential clue, the muff rolled away of its own accord. Then it began to *roll after him*, possessed by his wife's vengeful spirit. Terrified, the husband went to Detroit and confessed. Meanwhile the muff continued to roam the wastes. Reeking of the smell of death, the terrible "Rolling Muff" would chase after intruders in its accursed domain, supposedly as recently as the Prohibition era, when it supposedly affrighted some rumrunners.

More modern ghost lore claims that a bicycling boy in grey traverses roads through the Wildlife Sanctuary area of Grosse Ile. Motorists who pass the indistinct figure will look back to see nothing there. French-colonial traditions also describe the marshes of Grosse Ise as ablaze with treacherous SPOOK LIGHTS.

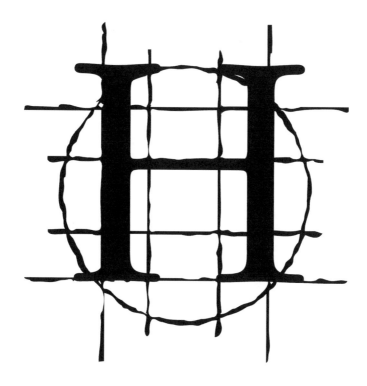

HALE, DENNIS (See *DANIEL J. MORRELL*)

HAMILTON **and** *SCOURGE* — Two Lake Ontario *Ghost Ships*, listed as casualties of the War of 1812, who shared identical fates in this world—and perhaps the next. The 112-foot *Hamilton* and the 108-foot *Scourge* were part of an American battle fleet of schooners, under Commodore Isaac Chauncey, sheltered at Niagara. In the early hours of August 8, 1813, as the Americans prepared for a fight with British ships, the calm, clear weather yielded to a fierce storm, and the *Hamilton* and the *Scourge* both sank in three hundred feet of water. Some of the crew were rescued, but most drowned; estimates of the fatalities ranged from fifty-three to nearly one hundred. Local tradition afterwards claimed that on foggy nights the two warships re-enact their last moments; the schooners under full sail and lantern lights, shuddering under the impact of an invisible storm and submerging. A sighting is taken as an OMEN of ill fortune. In 1942 sailors on board the steamship *Cayuga* reportedly saw the phantom vessels at dusk, and by morning, the *Cayuga's* steward had died.

The idea that the two old schooners may yet return has a basis in fact: since divers rediscovered the old ships they have been repeatedly revisited by scuba expeditions (including one by Jacques Cousteau in 1980). Explorers and researchers have pronounced the ships remarkably well preserved, and for twenty-five years discussions have been held on the feasibility of raising the ships to the surface again.

HARSENS ISLAND — An island resort and nature refuge on the St. Clair River, some twenty miles north of Detroit, where numerous GHOST stories center on and around a building that currently houses the Idle Hour Yacht Club. Originally built in 1891, it was a fishing and hunting club, a hotel (called the Riverside), and, during World War II, a training center for Coast Guardsmen. After a period of disuse, a new owner purchased and restored the building and grounds, and reopened it as the Idle Hour Yacht Club. Management admits to harboring a few ghosts; the spirits nicknamed *Annabelle*, *Jacob*, and '*Leisure Suit George*.' The legend of Leisure Suit George is that he was a guest from yesteryear who committed suicide in the old Riverside Hotel after his wife ran off with another man.

All three spirits are said to be extremely friendly and are veritable mascots of the place, blamed rather whimsically for any strange sounds or unusual occurrences, such as lights flickering on and off and doors mysteriously opening or, just as mysteriously, refusing to budge. The ghosts seem fond of oldies music and, in addition to untraceable dance music heard in the ballroom and bar in the off season, it's said that on occasion the old-fashioned forty-five-record jukebox will fire up and play selections all by itself—even when unplugged—and the unexplained odor of lilac perfumes pervades certain rooms. Children's voices have been heard in an otherwise empty game room. A "cold spot" lingers at the top of the stairway on the second floor.

In more than one anecdote, guests find themselves in conversation with staff or other visitors in old-fashioned garb, who subsequently, portentously vanish and cannot be traced to the register; in one case the description of a personable young maid matched that of a college girl who worked at the hotel in the 1960s and who died when her car ran into the river one night after her shift. A woman in white has been seen in the window of the otherwise empty bridal suite. Another venerable hunting club on Harsens Island, known simply as The Old Club, is said to house the spirit of a tall black man.

HENRY COURT (See JINXES and JONAHS)

HORSE ISLAND (See YEO ISLAND)

HUDSON — Author-historian Frederick Stonehouse relates a fisherman's yarn from Lake Superior that may rank as one of the most bizarre GHOST SHIP encounters on any sea. It sounds like something that should have been set down on foolscap by a quill pen under oil-lamp light in the 1500s—yet it purports to have occurred on the sixteenth day of September in the late 1940s. A fishing tug, rounding Keweenaw Point a few miles from shore, nearly ran into a badly rusted, steel-hulled, three hundred-foot ship in a thick mist. Apparently her engines were offline and she was adrift. When nobody responded to his hail, the tug's skipper hauled alongside and jumped onto the old steamship. He noted that her hatches were wooden (an archaic feature), her smokestacks askew, and her decks in terrible shape and awash in muck. Then he saw a crewman, a silent figure at a distance in sodden oilskins, who gestured that the visitor should go to the pilothouse. When he opened the door, the tug skipper saw two gaunt men with chalk-white faces and all-black eyes. They told him this was a ship of the living dead—the wreck of the steamer *Hudson*—lost with the entire crew of twenty-four in these very waters on September 16, 1901, with all hands, and cursed to reappear on the anniversary of the sinking. Advised by the accursed sailors that the time was short, the tug captain rushed back to his own boat in time to see the *Hudson* fade away. Immediately the skipper ordered the tug to seek shelter at Eagle Harbor, refusing to tell the first mate what had happened. The tug just escaped being swept up in the worst of a gale; it seems the phantom boat was an OMEN as well. Sadly, the wonderful tale names neither the skipper nor the tugboat involved.

HUNTER SAVIDGE — Author Frederick Stonehouse, long practiced at accounting Great Lakes GHOST SHIPS, calls this Lake Huron phantom one of the strangest of all because the tragic vessel appears to witnesses *inverted*—that is to say an upturned stern floating on the water.

The 117-foot, two-masted schooner sailed as part of a lumber company's small fleet. On her last earthly voyage—August 20, 1899—she was on a return trip from shuttling coal between Sarnia, Ontario, and Alpena, Michigan. Mary Mullerwiess, wife of company owner John Mullerwiess, had been feeling ill and went along on the trip with her six-year-old daughter, Etta, to recover her health on the late-summer lake. Instead a sudden squall caught the ship and capsized her. Captain Fred Sharpstreen and four of his crew were hurled off the decks into the water, where they clung helplessly to wreckage until picked up by the nearby steamer *Alexander McVittie*. Captain Sharpsteen tried to persuade the crew of the *McVittie* to immediately hack into the exposed hull of the *Hunter Savidge*, still bobbing above the waterline; Sharpsteen's own wife had also been aboard and a missing crewman was his own sixteen-year-old son.

In exceptional cases of similar capsizing incidents, survivors had managed to remain alive, in trapped air bubbles in holds, sometimes for days, before being freed, and Captain Sharpsteen held out hope some of the missing family members might still be rescued. But the master of the *Alexander McVittie*, with a schedule to keep, steamed away, handing off the remaining personnel of the *Hunter Savidge* crew to another ship, which took them to a lifesaving station at Sand Beach. By then night had fallen—too late to set out again for the bobbing wreck, if indeed the schooner were still afloat. When Sharpsteen finally chartered a tugboat to search for the *Hunter Savidge*, he could find no trace of her. Nor did any other searchers, despite months of looking. Confounding the mystery were contradictory reports that the half-submerged boat was seen in other locations. The bereaved Sharpsteen was very vocal in the maritime press about his treatment by the *McVittie* and the lives that might have been saved.

Perhaps it is as a consequence and a cautionary tale about letting bureaucracy and commerce rule over mercy. But the ghostly legends claimed that on foggy nights on Lake Huron sailors might still catch a glimpse of the upturned hull, its prisoners waiting for release that never came. In 1987 divers identified the wreck of the lost schooner on the lake bottom 155 feet down.

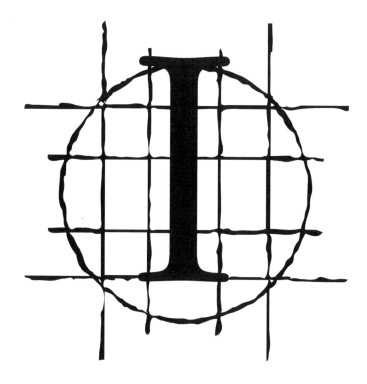

IDLE HOUR YACHT CLUB (See HARSENS ISLAND)

IGOPOGO — Name given a reputed LAKE MONSTER dwelling in Lake Simcoe, a large Canadian lake between Lake Huron's Georgian Bay and Lake Ontario; it's connected to both lakes via rivers. The name of the monster declares, phonetically, a tie to a more famous and frequently sighted creature in western Canada's Lake Okanagan, 'Ogopogo.' The Lake Simcoe creature has been given varying descriptions—some sound snakelike, others tell of a rather appealing dog-faced animal with a neck similar to an old-fashioned stove-pipe—and has been spotted by many people over the past one hundred years, particularly in the south end of the lake and the deep waters of Kempenfelt Bay. Residents of Beaverton, on the eastern shore, call it 'Beaverton Bessie,' while others refer to it as 'Kempenfelt Kelly.'

Sources refer vaguely to early INDIAN LEGENDS of the monster and sporadic reports of a "sea serpent" in the lake during the nineteenth century. Important sightings occurred in 1952 and 1963, and a "sonar sounding of a large animal" was made in 1983. Measurements given by observers are wildly inconsistent, putting

Igopogo's length at anywhere from twelve to seventy feet. A 1963 sighting (witnesses included a Presbyterian minister) claimed Igopogo had dorsal fins, despite it having distinctly mammalian characteristics that suggest it could be a wandering seal or sea lion from the St. Lawrence Seaway. Reportedly Igopogo was caught on amateur videotape in 1991, surfacing near a distressed boater. The very few who have studied the footage rendered an opinion that it indeed shows an inquisitive seal. The shoreline of Lake Simcoe, near the town of Brechin, is also supposed to be haunted by a moving SPOOK LIGHT.

INDIAN LEGENDS — The tribal folk belief and religious stories, sorcery, and myths of the Great Lakes' indigenous peoples have intermingled with the ghostly tales and yarns told by European settlers. Even late twentieth century authors seeking credence for their published volumes on UFOS and USOS or TRIANGLES and VORTICES have made highly selective citations of native lore, interpreting accounts of shamans who could fly in the sky or a once-mighty kingdom near Wisconsin, now vanished, as eyewitness confirmation of ancient aviators, or an Atlantis-style lost civilization of tremendous power.

Many of the native legends obviously personify storms, waves, WEATHER ANOMALIES, and other naturally occurring phenomena, especially from the vicinity of the upper lakes, on the shores of Michigan

and Wisconsin, where ore deposits tended to attract a large number of lightning strikes. Ancient Chippewa superstition particularly assign the temperament of troubled waters to various forms of Lake Monsters, echoing the claims of Canadian Indians to the west that a long-necked underwater menace called Naitaka would drown and devour men and deer foolhardy enough to venture into its feeding-grounds. Nameless—but very often cited as Great Lakes Indian folklore—is the giant sturgeon in Lake Superior. The colossal fish is capable of swallowing a whole ship. It can, with the flick of a fin, churn into boiling violence a small spot on the surface of the lake. Many Chippewa braves have seen either the fish or clear evidence of it. Nanabazhoo, a comical hero in Chippewa mythology, was once swallowed by the sturgeon, but escaped through his guile. When canoes went out on the Superior to fish and never came back, it was said they had fallen prey to the sturgeon and not been so resourceful as Nanabazhoo.

Another Ojibway monster of Lake Superior, with similar destructive tendencies, is Mishipishu (also known to Potawatomi tribes as "Nampe-shiu," who placed its habitat as Lake Geneva in Wisconsin). Mishipishu was said to be a gigantic lynx or panther (though in painted representations, curiously dinosaur-like, with ridges of spines down his back), whose great tail could swipe away an entire village. Mishipishu was said to be especially protective of the sacred copper deposits of ISLE ROYALE and MICHIPICOTEN ISLAND. Yet another Lake Superior creature, or perhaps a variation on the Mishipishu, was Mishi Ginabig,

described as more snakelike. The enemy of Mishi Ginabig was the Thunderbird, and there is a story that in the 1800s a decisive battle erupted between the pair, which ended with the Thunderbird lifting Mishi Ginabig out of the water and into the sky to disappear for good. Indians witnessed a powerful lightning strike on the west shore of Lake Superior that they took as evidence of this fight. Another important concept, the WINDIGO or Wendigo, was the very personification of hunger and starvation, an evil force that could possess and drive people to the madness of cannibalism.

Nineteenth century engraving depicting the European view of North American Indians.

More concrete and still evident to modern eyes (though in sometimes precarious states of existence) are the scattered petroglyphs and natural formations that comprise sacred sites throughout the lakes. Here holy men would go on "vision quests" or contemplate Gitchee Manitou (in the language of the Algonquins), the powerful Great Spirit and Master of Life, present in all things, and his negative/evil counterpart, Matchi Manitou (or sometimes Mackee Monedo). The limestone formation "Arch Rock" on MACKINAC ISLAND was a gateway through which the Manitou would pass. Sacred Rock, on the shore of Lake Huron, six miles north of Rogers City, Michigan, is a distinctive ten-foot glacial boulder, a scene of Ojibway animal sacrifices and offerings in the past. Tribal legend states two chiefs from feuding tribes were quarreling here so much so that they annoyed the Gitchee Manitou, who put a stop to their fracas by either smashing them beneath the rock or sending a lightning bolt to smite the rock on which they both stood. When rain washed over Sacred Rock, the blood of the men would become visible again. Inscription Rock, at Agaway Bay, Ontario, holds a variety of mystical Ojibway rock paintings. For a century the rock itself, first described by white man in 1851, was thought to have been a myth, its exact location lost, but native-art specialist Selwyn Dewdney rediscovered it in 1959. Sanilac Petroglyph State Park in Huron County, Michigan, holds a fragile, soft-sandstone rock filled with carvings, thought to be a place of meditation for the ancestors of the Chippewa.

Such petroglyphs represent the only form of Indian "writing"; much of today's inadequate perspective into the beliefs and rituals of the original Great Lakes inhabitants derives from the journals of early Jesuit missionaries. They describe a magical ceremony known as the "Shaking Tent," in which a wigwam-style tent would be erected, apparently stout, and fixed firmly in the earth. An Indian medicine man, sometimes described as old and frail looking and naked or nearly naked, would enter this tent and begin chanting. Eventually, the whole tent would twist and contort violently, sparks and fire flying out the aperture at the top, and different voices would be heard as the shaman received an audience with the Manitou. When the ceremony ended, all that the tent contained was the exhausted medicine man. Some white witness considered the Shaking Tent a basic conjuring trick, comparable to ventriloquism and contrived as pulling a rabbit from a top hat. Others were impressed and thought paranormal forces were indeed at work here in this untamed new world.

(See also BELLE ISLE, BETE GRIS, DEVIL'S CHAIR, DEVIL'S ISLAND, ISLE ROYALE, KAKABEKA FALLS, MAID OF THE MIST, MANITOULIN ISLAND, MICHIPICOTEN ISLAND, PUKASKWA, ONNIONT, ROCKMAN, and THUNDERBIRD)

IOSCO (See *OLIVE JEANETTE*)

IRONSIDES — A plush passenger steamer, 218 feet long and 937 tons, built by Quayle and Martin and launched July 23, 1864 in Cleveland, Ohio, she had forty-four staterooms, expensive carpeting, chandeliers, and the novelty of hot and cold running water, earning her the designation "palace steamer." Though basically wooden, metal plating may have reinforced her hull, though contemporary records are unclear on this. What is clear is the irony that, despite a name denoting sturdiness, both she and her sister ship *Lac La Belle* would be Lake Michigan shipwrecks before logging even ten years' service.

The *Ironsides* operated out of Cleveland with runs to Lake Superior, Detroit, and MACKINAC ISLAND. In 1869 the *Ironsides* and Lac *La Belle* were sold to the Englemann Transportation Company from Milwaukee, Wisconsin, and switched to routes that took her from Milwaukee to the important railroad terminals of Grand Haven, Michigan. Modern Great Lake historian Wes Oleszewski has made the case that the Engelmann Transportation was guilty of penny-pinching and negligence in the proper maintenance of its vessels, even though the *Ironsides* supposedly underwent a thorough overhaul in late 1872, after the October 14, 1872 loss of the *Lac la Belle*, which sank off Racine, Wisconsin after leaving Milwaukee for Grand Haven, Michigan. Though pronounced in excellent condition, it would be a mere eleven months later, on September 14, 1873, that the *Ironsides* also met her doom. She left Milwaukee at 9:45 p.m. with nineteen passengers and a crew of thirty, carrying 13,000 bushels of wheat, five hundred barrels of flour, 125 barrels of pork, and other merchandise (including, as wreck divers later discovered, costumes and props of a theatrical troupe). A moderate southwest breeze was blowing and turned overnight into a full gale. The *Ironsides* began to take on water, though at the inquest the company offered contradictory testimony that there was no leak. Water overwhelmed the engine room, snuffing out "Jack" and "Jill," the two giant steam turbines. Survivors thought Captain Harry Sweetman—who did not live through the voyage and was consequently blamed by the company for the disaster—was trying to bring the ship through the Grand Haven channel to safety, but Oleszewski thought they were misinterpreting the ship's turning helplessly in the huge waves. By 9 a.m. the ship started sinking and five lifeboats launched; Captain Sweetman being, by custom, the last to leave. Only two of the lifeboats reached shore; the others capsized in rough water, as the *Ironsides'* decks came apart and she submerged in 120 feet of Lake Michigan around the noon hour. Newspaper accounts are slightly confused over the number of fatalities, putting the death toll as high as twenty-one, including Captain Sweetman and Chief Engineer Robert McGlue. Englemann Transportation announced plans to raise the wreck from the bottom, but never did. Wreck divers rediscovered the *Ironsides* in the 1960s.

The postscript in a form of a GHOST story takes place in early August 2000 during a weeklong anniversary celebration of the Coast Guard, off Grand Haven. A thick fog had settled over the area and the crew of the icebreaker *Mackinaw* clearly heard a voice, apparently that of a small boy, crying out in the distance for help. A thorough and careful sweep was made of the vicinity, with a second Coast Guard boat joining in. The crying voice was heard repeatedly by the guardsmen (yet not by any of the pleasure-boating civilians also on the water at the time). The source was never determined. Wes Oleszewski links the pathetic cries for help to the loss of the *Ironsides* in this same region more than a century earlier and the fact that a little child, one Harry Valentine, was among the passengers who did not come ashore alive.

ISLE OF COVES LIGHTHOUSE (See COVE ISLAND LIGHT)

ISLE ROYALE — An island in Lake Superior, forty-four miles long and four to nine miles wide, it's surrounded by dangerous shoals on which many a ship has run aground. The island has significant copper-mining works, some very ancient, dated long before white settlement or known Indian history. Lore among the Chippewa is said to include the notion that a curse of vague origin was placed upon the precious copper deposits, and that ill fortune befalls those who seek to remove the mineral from the island. And indeed, Douglass Houghton, the first white man to spread the word about the fabulous copper, drowned straightaway in a canoe accident at the age of thirty-four, earning him posthumous fame in a tragic ballad.

Certainly some of the bad luck ascribed to the curse could be attributed to the hordes of tenderfoot speculators and poorly provisioned profiteers who flocked to the remote, inhospitable island when the copper rush began in 1845. Isle Royale is now a national park, with park headquarters on Mott Island, which is named for the Motts, Angelique, a Christianized Indian maiden, and her husband Charlie (Charles LaMotte) a French *voyageur*. In 1845 they were persuaded to stay at Isle Royale alone by a copper speculator, who then apparently failed to dispatch proper supplies for the long, bitter winter. Charlie went mad from hunger and starved to death, and Angelique survived to tell gruesome stories about resisting the urge to eat him.

A later casualty of the "curse of the copper" singled out by historian Dwight Boyer was the *Kitty Reeves*, a three-masted schooner laden with a fortune in copper from Isle Royale, which had to be abandoned by her captain and crew during a fierce November gale on Lake Huron in 1870. The ship's anchor snapped and she drifted before being overwhelmed by the waves somewhere near Tawas Point. Salvagers spent much of the next century hunting for her copper-laden sunken wreck, supposedly buried under tons of shifting sand. Hikers on Isle Royale have been recommended (somewhat facetiously) a spooky time by going on the Windigo Nature Trail, named, of course, for the threatening (and, in echo of the Motts, sometimes cannibalistic) spirit of Indian Legends. It is said that if you turn a detailed map of Isle Royale upside down, you will see the image of a flying demon, but this is very much in the eye of the beholder.

Among the many shipwrecks in the Isle Royale vicinity with noteworthy GHOST traditions is the *Emperor*. The Menagerie Island Lighthouse, on a small rocky outcrop off Isle Royale's southern shore, is not the only lighthouse here, but it's often referred to as the Isle Royale Lighthouse. The tower was built in 1875 and longtime keeper John Malone became regionally famous as a hunter and guide from the late 1800s to the early 1900s. He and his wife raised thirteen children on Isle Royale, and it has been claimed that visitors still see the spirit of one of the young Malone boys, who slipped on the rocks and died. The Rock of Ages Lighthouse, erected on an isolated shoal of Isle Royale and illuminated in 1908, has also been called haunted, but is off-limits to the general public.

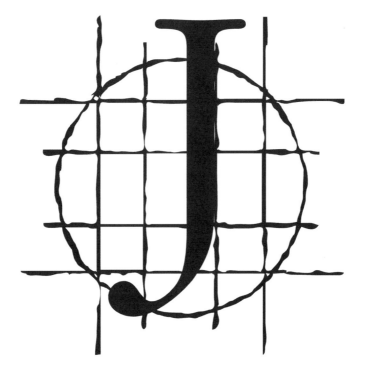

JANE MILLER — A seventy-eight-foot, 218-foot coastal passenger steamship built on MANITOULIN ISLAND and serving nearby ports in the Georgian Bay region of Lake Huron. On November 25, 1885, she was running lumber and travelers from Big Bay to Wiarton when she disappeared in a storm, leaving no survivors and just minimal wreckage...an ideal precursor for the legend of a GHOST SHIP. However, it was not a "sighting" that listed her in the logbook of the supernatural, but rather a *hearing*. In autumn of 1906, a hunting party camped for the night on Georgian Bay's White Cloud Island reported distant cries for help traveling over the storm-tossed waters. In the blackness they could make out no ship in distress, and bad weather prevented them from launching their own small boat to investigate. No source for the screams was determined, and Great Lakes lore has concluded that the ghostly victims of the *Jane Miller* sinking had been replaying the tragedy close to its anniversary.

JAVA and JENNIE GRAHAM (See SHIP NAMES)

JINXES and JONAHS — Seagoing SUPERSTITION is replete with stories of vessels that seemingly toiled under a curse,

A ship launching, shown here in a vintage engraving, was a crucial occasion on which a JINX might announce itself.

or longstanding bad luck, as a result of some transgression or violation of a taboo. Coleridge's "Rime of the Ancient Mariner" is the classic expression in verse of a ship at sea so condemned, as well as apocryphal yarns about the *Titanic* or the *Great Eastern*; that their regrettable destinies could be traced to a workman, killed or overlooked, and accidentally sealed up alive in a hull compartment during the final welding. On the Great Lakes, a folkloric equivalent may well be the *ERIE BOARD OF TRADE*, a (very likely fictitious) schooner plagued by BOTH a ghost and a sentence of *doom* because of a captain's rash orders causing the death of a crewmember.

Also unique to the lakes is the foggy curse said to hover over the copper deposits of ISLE ROYALE and Upper Michigan territories. Mined by some unknown prehistoric civilization and later sacred to Indian tribes, the ore is said to be protected by a misfortune visited upon those who covet the copper; hence the fates of the *PEWABIC* and *METEOR*, among others.

Numerous are the *ship names* said to convey ill fortune, and Great Lakes sailors of yesteryear would disdain having either women or cats on board...for fear of *invoking* a jinx. But some jinx or "hoodoo" ships do not seem to have committed such obvious offenses. Merely being "born bad" or launched under an unlucky star is enough, as in the case of the *Erie Wave*, a Canadian schooner that capsized on her first two trips, each time causing two deaths, until her final wreck—from which only two of all those aboard survived.

Jinxed Ships

• The ***Anna C Minch***, a steel freighter launched in 1903, gained a reputation as a "bad luck craft" after suffering a dozen collisions with other ships and piers between 1907 and 1925 and stranding in Lake Michigan. In 1940 she received a mortal wound during a Lake Michigan storm. Something put a hole in her bow and she sank in forty feet of water off Pentwater, the crew perishing. It was long assumed that the Anna *C Minch* had impaled herself on the wreck of an earlier steamer, the *William B Davock*, but divers inspecting the scene later claimed the *Davock* showed no sign of such a disturbance.

• The ***Troy***, a 163-foot wooden steamer launched in 1849, suffered a litany of collisions, sinkings, and groundings. Between 1850 and 1856 her boiler exploded twice, each time killing several crewmen. Finally, in October 1859, the *Troy*, carrying passengers and a cargo of wheat from Racine, Wisconsin, to Port Colborne, Ontario, was battered by a ferocious Lake Huron storm. The order was given to abandon ship and the bulk of the refugees crowded into a large lifeboat. Three of the crew were late in departing and took their chances instead in a leaky old yawl; ironically, they were the lone survivors.

• The ***Walter H. Oades***: "One of the most unlucky vessels on the lakes," went an 1888 newspaper epitaph for the schooner. While under construction in Detroit, she was almost destroyed by fire; her launching was botched; early in her service she ran aground; under later owners she was rammed by a steamboat on the St. Clair River; she hit a break wall in Buffalo—and those were only the most serious accidents recorded. Far more numerous were the minor ones. At the time of her final wrecking, the *Walter H. Oades* carried no insurance because no company wanted to take the risk.

• One of the most curious jinxes was said to hang over an entire shipping firm, the **Minnesota Atlantic Transit Company**. Their line was known as the "Poker Fleet" because of a whim of the managers to name their vessels after types of playing cards—*King, Queen, Ace, Jack, Ten,* and *Nine*. It was noticed, however, that the hand of fate dealt to captains of the Poker fleet was a grim one. Captain James McDonald was on his way to board the *Ace* in Duluth when he was hit and killed by a car. Another Minnesota Atlantic Transit captain died in a car accident in Detroit, and another perished in World War II when his ship convoy was torpedoed. On October 29, 1951, Captain Louis Guyette, who had served in the Poker Fleet and now commanded the cargo ship *Penobscot*, died in an inferno after the *Penobscot*'s nocturnal collision with a barge laden with gasoline tanks, in a narrow channel where the Buffalo River empties into Lake Erie.

Because of the Great Lakes' unique configuration, "lake boats," especially the giant freighters, came to be designed along different lines than their ocean-going counterparts, often lying lower and heavier in the water. Nautical engineers the world over have had lively arguments about the structural virtues and drawbacks, about which ships are stronger in any given extreme-storm conditions. The inland seas' ship-building factories even produced one bizarre variety of boat unique to the Great Lakes and nowhere else—the "whaleback"—which looked like a boat's deck on top of a round-edged steel hull, similar in appearance to a giant submarine. No more than forty whalebacks were launched. Detractors claimed they had a certain resemblance to enormous pigs.

• The **Henry Cort** was a "whaleback"-design freighter launched in 1892 under the name *Pillsbury*. A steel hauler for much of her career, she gained a reputation for bad luck. Struck by a steamer in December 1917, she sank and was raised at great cost the next year to be sent on more misadventures before she hit a break wall off Muskegon, Michigan, in 1934. In a curious confluence of jinxes, author Frederick Stonehouse has said that the thirty-six-foot motor lifeboat used by the Michigan Coast Guard in getting to the *Henry Court* had also earned a reputation for unmanageability throughout her "lifesaving" career. During the rescue operation, she overturned and a twenty-three-year-old rookie Guardsman drowned (though the twenty-five-man crew of the *Henry Court* were rescued).

• Being a jinx ship did not necessarily mean being unpopular. The **Tashmoo**, a three hundred-foot side-wheel steamer launched auspiciously on December 30, 1899, was a plushy appointed favorite for excursionists on the Detroit River and a competitor in a famous one hundred-mile race on Lake Erie in 1901 against rival passenger ship *City of Erie* (the *Tashmoo* lost). In her later years, however, the *Tashmoo* careened from one disaster to another, colliding with a ferry in a 1927 storm; running aground in 1934; and hitting a submerged obstruction in the Detroit River in 1936. Clumsy salvage operations this last time damaged her beyond repair, but her ornate pilothouse was removed and converted by its buyer into an unusual summer cottage. But in 1951 even that remnant caught fire and burned to the ground.

Jonahs

While some vessels are said to be jinxes, there are also some people said to carry ill fortune aboard with them. These ambulatory curses are dubbed "Jonahs," after the Biblical prophet swallowed by the whale. Historian Frederick Stonehouse has tabulated a number of sailors and captains who worked one ship after another that came to grief, including a certain Captain Martin Daniels, who experienced no fewer than nine shipwrecks in twenty-two years (eight on the open oceans and one on the Great Lakes).

A sailor named E. H. Shoemaker was a veteran of four shipwrecks when, in 1902, the whaleback on which he was serving, the *Thomas Wilson*, collided with a wooden steamer, *George G. Hadley*, on Lake Superior near Duluth. Shoemaker and the other men of the *Wilson* scrambled aboard the *Hadley*, which still seemed seaworthy. While making to safety, however, the *Hadley* herself submerged. Once again Shoemaker survived. It seems a glass half-empty/half-full dichotomy over whether the likes of Daniels and Shoemaker are unnaturally unlucky or providentially fortunate in being able to escape from so many disasters.

One sailor singled out in the news media as a Jonah during his active career was Captain Walter R. Neal. In November 1919, the thirty-seven-year veteran of the lakes was commanding the 180-foot wooden steamer *Myron*, towing the *Miztec*, a barge filled with lumber, when she was blasted by a Lake Superior winter storm. Though Neal cut the barge loose, the *Myron* was doomed. Even with rescue ships fighting to reach the wreckage all the crew who evacuated in a lifeboat died in the cold. Only Captain Neal, who had remained aboard the Myron, survived by clinging to the floating pilothouse. So narrow an escape had the 54-year-old enjoying that newspapers in his hometown falsely reported his death, and Neal was especially vocal in condemning the ships that had failed to save his men. But in 1920 Captain Neal made news again as the officer in charge of a 201-foot steamer *Charles H. Bradley.* That summer on Lake Huron, with the Bradley again towing the *Miztec* and another barge, the *Mary Woolson* with cargoes of salt, a squall blew up, and the *Mary Woolson* suddenly rammed the *Charles H. Bradley* in the stern. It was the barge that sustained the worse damage and sunk, and Captain Neal deliberately beached the *Bradley* at Alapena to avoid her submerging. Then in 1921, Neal was first mate aboard the steamer *Zillah* — again towing the *Miztec* — when the salt-loaded barge was struck by a spring snowstorm several miles from Whitefish Point, Lake Superior. The *Miztec* broke free and sank, its crew of six lost, not far from where the *Myron* had wrecked. In the summer of 1926 the aging *Zillah* herself sank, also near Whitefish Point.

While contemporary newspapers commented on "the Captain's jinx," it must be added that Captain Walter R. Neal died peacefully in Bay City, Michigan, in 1951, at age 86. Great Lakes historian and wreck diver Cris Kohl points out several other ships on which he served logged no exceptional strife, and that the *Myron* seemed to suffer frequent misfortune and mishaps before he became her master. In fact, the *Myron* had earlier been known as the *Mark Hopkins* until her owner rechristened her after his son, thus violating a ship-name taboo.

(See also: *AUGUSTA* and *LADY ELGIN*, *CHICORA*, and *OLIVE JEANETTE*)

JOHN OWEN (See THREE-FINGERED REILLY)

JOHNSONS ISLAND — A Lake Erie island in the western side of the lake, it's near Sandusky between Cleveland and Toledo, two miles from the Ohio shores. It is unusual that a northern outpost such as this played a role in the Civil War, but it did, and from that arises a GHOST story. Johnsons Island is separated from Sandusky by two miles of lake that freezes over in the winter, providing a convenient, if uncomfortable, overland route. During the War Between the

States, this three hundred-acre spot was designated by the Union to be a natural holding pen for Confederate officers and high-risk prisoners. The lake and twelve-foot stockade walls would contain them. Between 10,000 and 15,000 southerners were interned here, and remarkably, a few actually did manage to escape. Many more rebels suffered the bleak, unaccustomed chill, resulting in epidemics of pneumonia and fever. An estimated 206 men died here and were buried with temporary wooden markers.

In the early years of the twentieth century, the United Daughters of the Confederacy worked to make the cemetery on Johnsons Island a resting place of military honor and distinction, with marble headstones and statuary. The story goes that a crew of about 150 Italian quarrymen was digging for the limestone deposits on Johnsons Island not long after the erection of the monuments in 1915 when a March storm blew up. Driven to the remains of the stockade by the tempest, the workmen reported seeing the new, heroic statue of a Confederate actually *move* to face the graves — and blow reveille. Then the men beheld misty, glowing shapes of deceased soldiers rising, shouldering arms, and marching away to the next world. The Italians recalled the song sung by the legion of phantoms. The witnesses could only repeat the melody since they spoke little or no English, and the song was unfamiliar to them. It was "Dixie." The laborers refused to return to work after what they had experienced.

JOSEPH A. HOLLON — A wooden barge, 107 foot, 158 gross tons, built in 1867 at East Saginaw, Michigan. On October 30, 1870, she was in tow of the tug *Clematis* in a gale on Lake Huron. The barge broke free and drifted off. Waves washed the captain overboard, and the pounding surf destroyed the cabins. A total of four crewmen died, while another (and the wife of the first mate) escaped somehow on board a bark that conveyed them to Detroit. Five days after the storm, the vessel was found adrift twenty-five miles southwest of POINT AUX BARQUES, off Bay Port, and was towed into Port Elgin, Ontario, with the grisly detail that one last crew member had manned the ship in the worst way, "lashed to a pump, dead, with his eyes picked out" by carrion gulls. This last gruesome detail resurfaced (perhaps inevitably) in an account collected by Great Lakes historian Wes Oleszewski. It claimed that in the 1960s an auto worker, fishing from his boat off Bay Port, got a fright of his life when he spotted at close range the *Joseph A. Hollon* as a GHOST SHIP — a battered and broken derelict with the eyeless corpse of the nineteenth century crewman plainly visible on deck.

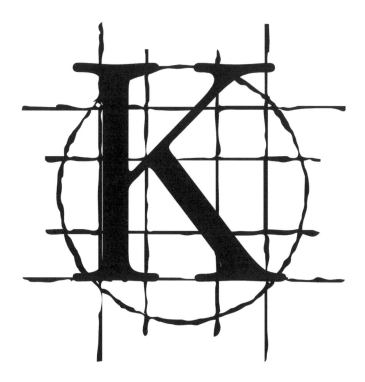

KAKABEKA FALLS — An INDIAN LEGEND involves this scenic waterfall on the Canadian side of Lake Superior, on the Kaministiquia River at Thunder Bay. The name (shared by a nearby town) derives from a corruption of the Ojibway name meaning "waterfall over a cliff." The tale told involves an Ojibwe princess named Green Mantle, asked by her aged chieftain father White Bear to help defend against a war-party of Sioux. Princess Green Mantle, pretending to be lost, entered the Sioux camp along the Kaministiquia River and begged the invaders to spare her life; in return she promised to lead them to White Bear. Placed at the head of a canoe, Green Mantle instead directed the Sioux warriors toward the waterfall, where they all tumbled to their deaths, sparing the Ojibway from an assault. Legend claims that one can see Green Mantle in the mist of Kakabeka Falls, or in the rainbow caused by the falls — a mystic tribute awarded the heroine by the great spirit Gitchee Manitou in return for her sacrifice. Meanwhile the angry cries of the Sioux warriors echoes in the roar of the water. Other slightly less tragic versions of the story say she blundered across the approaching Sioux purely by accident, made up the plan on the spot, and jumped out of the canoe and swam to shore safely, leaving the enemy to go over the falls. Kakabeka Falls

The scenic KAKABEKA FALLS on Lake Superior, a cascade linked to an INDIAN LEGEND. *Photo copyright by Sylvia Banks.*

is sometimes compared to Niagara Falls for its visual majesty, and the similarities between the Green Mantle narrative and the better-known MAID OF THE MIST tradition is strong indeed.

KALIYUGA — A 280-foot wooden freighter built by the Simon Langell shipyard in St. Clair, Michigan in 1887, it was purchased by the Cleveland Cliffs Iron Company. *Omens* of a grim fate awaiting her are said to date back to August 1897. While the ship was engulfed in a thick fog on Lake Huron, miles from shore, crewmen claimed to have heard something like howling, or a dog barking and growling, on board—though the ship carried no such mascot. An even weirder story puts the *Kaliyuga* again fogbound on Lake Superior two years later. Supposedly a deckhand saw an exact double of the ship running alongside, just thirty feet away—complete with an ominous duplicate of himself, who answered the man's hails by holding up a cardboard sign on which was written "GET OFF THE SHIP." When the *Kaliyuga* reached her destination, the port of Detroit, the deckhand fled. In late October 1905, the *Kaliyuga* left Marquette, Michigan, with a load of ore for Cleveland. She ran into a storm and sank with no survivors and bodies and debris from the pilothouse floating. Later sailor talk claimed the *Kaliyuga* could be seen (and heard) as a GHOST SHIP near Presque Isle in stormy weather, still blowing her horn in alarm as she fights the waves.

KARSTEN INN — Located in the Lake Michigan shoreline community of Kewaunee, Wisconsin, this historic 1912 inn is said to be *very busy with* GHOSTS. Paranormal phenomena were first reported during renovations in the 1960s. Manifestations include cold spots, moving or vanishing tools, strange noises (one especially sounding like an old-fashioned whisk broom sweeping), pungent odors, and apparitions of a maid in an archaic costume (once glimpsed in an old mirror). Alleged psychics have diagnosed three spirits as being responsible. One of the ghosts is identified as German immigrant William 'Big Bill' Karsten, Sr.; a Great Lakes crewman nicknamed the 'Old Sailor,' who also was once elected mayor of the town. He died in 1940 at age seventy-eight, in room 210. A later owner of the property heard wheezing and gasping breaths in that room.

Big Bill is blamed for rearranging furniture and perpetrating mischief on the housekeeping staff. Other phenomena include toilets flushing and water running by itself, sounds of breaking glass and flute music, and invisible children playing and crying. A mysterious, evasive little boy who plays with children of guests has been attributed to the spirit of Karsten's grandson, who died from meningitis not long after his grandfather. The maid, nicknamed 'Agatha,' is supposedly a local woman who worked at the inn and might have been Big Bill's lover. The Karsten Inn opened to the public as a restaurant in May 2001, and guest books record plentiful anecdotes about strange noises interpreted as possible Agatha encounters. The Inn is located at the intersection of Ellis and Lake Streets.

KELLEYS ISLAND — A large, shield-shaped island north of Sandusky and the Marblehead Peninsula in Lake Erie and a favorite visitation site for tourists and boaters, it bears both glacial groves from the elemental forces that gouged out the Great Lakes and a famous "Inscription Rock" set of petroglyphs left by prehistoric peoples. Limestone quarrying was a major industry here. A GHOST story is told resulting from a nineteenth century cave-in due to unwise blasting at the limestone tunnels, which caused a collapse that killed numerous men, mostly immigrant Italian laborers. Because the same company that owned the mine ran much of the industrial traffic on Lake Erie, the trapped spirits of the dead men took revenge on passing ships for decades afterwards, right up to the 1930s, sinking the boats that passed over their subterranean tomb. The spirits of the drowned sailors also added to the number of restless dead. Tall tales claimed that the limestone tunnels in which these angry ghosts were trapped nearly spanned the ten miles to the Marblehead Peninsula shore.

KEMPENFELT KELLY (See IGOPOGO)

KEYSTONE STATE — A wooden side-wheel steamer, carrying both passengers and cargo, she was built in 1849 in Buffalo and embarked in November 1861 on her first trip after a five-year lay-up. Her route was to take her from Detroit to Milwaukee, with passengers, "hardware," and even a rumored shipment of gold. She never arrived, last seen in a gale on Lake Huron, near Port Austin, Michigan. Wreckage was seen off POINT AUX BARQUES on November 21 and her wheelhouse washed ashore a few days later. She was said to have been sighted subsequently as a GHOST SHIP, which is probably cold comfort to the thirty-three lives lost when she went down.

KINGSTIE — An affectionate name given to a LAKE MONSTER of eastern Lake Ontario, which is said to be partial to the waters around Kingston, Ontario, and the mouth of the St. Lawrence River. Sightings of the Kingstie supposedly date back to the early nineteenth century. There was an 1817 account of a great eel-like creature in the lake, watched by a schooner's crew. In 1887 the monster allegedly "raced" and outpaced a passenger steamer, *Gypsy*. Witnesses put the creature's length at up to forty-five feet, with small legs and a large tail. Encounters with Kingstie tend to have the flavor of fanciful newspaper hoaxes of the era, such as the 1892 allegation that a husband and wife in a skiff off Brakey's Bay were attacked by a monster serpent "with eyes like balls of fire," which the man repelled, beating it with his fishing pole. Similarly sensational is the description in a well-publicized Kingstie sighting by two physicians in a sailboat in August 1931: a thirty-foot leviathan with but one eye in the middle of its forehead and antler-like horns.

In 1979 some local men claimed to have perpetrated Kingstie sightings in the 1930s using a mock monster created out of floating bottles in Cartwright Bay. Nonetheless, rumors of large, unknown animals in the area continue to trickle in, most recently in 2004.

KINROSS INCIDENT — From the files of UFOS and USOS comes this allegation of a fatal flying saucer encounter over Lake Superior on November 23, 1953. An F-89C "Scorpion" Interceptor jet left Kinross Air Force Base near the Soo Locks in Michigan's Upper Peninsula to investigate a "bogey" or unknown aircraft detected via radar. Ground controllers followed the progress of the nocturnal pursuit, as the jet chased the 500-mph UFO to 8,000 feet, seventy miles off Keweenaw Point, while escalating static disrupted radio communications. At close to midnight the blip and the jet appeared to merge on the radar scope, and the plane and its two crewmen,

Highly suspicious "sidescan sonar" images that alleged to show wreckage of a plane/flying saucer collision, the KINROSS INCIDENT.

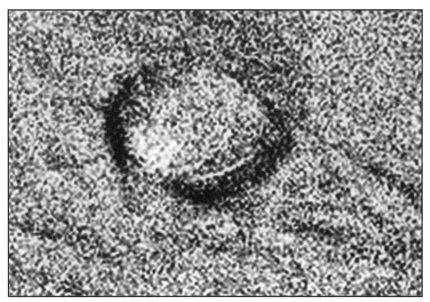

pilot Felix Moncla and radar observer Robert Wilson, were never seen again...*at least not by human eyes*.

The official explanation was that the pair had simply found a Canadian plane, identified in some records as a Royal Canadian Air Force C47 (and in other stories simply as a "Canadian airliner") flying from Winnipeg to Sudbury, Canada. Following this fairly routine contact, Moncla had suffered some sort of disorientation and crashed into the lake. This verdict was unacceptable to popular authors in the UFO community, who countered that the Canadian government denied any of their craft were in the vicinity; that Moncla could easily have switched to autopilot, or even ejected safely; that no floating wreckage or oil slicks were found after an extensive search the next day; and that ground-radar personnel and media reports were straightaway hushed up. It may be relevant that a second F-89C — belonging to the same squadron — crashed that same day during a test flight, calling into serious question the safety of this type of aircraft. Nonetheless, UFO-conspiracy buffs continued to speak of the unsolved "Kinross Incident" or "Kinross Case" as one in which a solid-object UFO radar image "swallowed" a hapless US military warplane and its two men.

Some interest in the case arose again in the saucer subculture in 2006, when an enterprise called the Great Lakes Diving Company announced high-tech side-scan sonar images showing an F-89C with minor collision damage half-buried on the bottom of Lake Superior—and a dented, disc-shaped object resting nearby. Even some UFO researchers suspected a deception, pointing out the unlikelihood of the F-89C being so remarkably intact. The company claimed it was keeping the location a secret, pending funds to send robotic submersibles down and produce a tie-in documentary, with company spokesmen complaining of interference from Canadian authorities and the US Coast Guard. Background checks revealed no evidence of a "Great Lakes Diving Company" as a registered business, and the firm's website (soon to do a vanishing act itself) was traced to an elusive California man, not any location in the Great Lakes region. It would seem doubtless that the affair was a hoax; the "sonar" images probably doctored digital snapshots of hobby-kit models on a fake lake bottom.

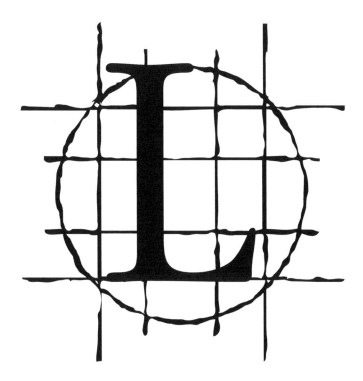

LA LLORONA — A mythic GHOST of Hispanic folk belief, whose legend has migrated across the Atlantic Ocean to become particularly prevalent in Mexico and Latin America and throughout parts of the United States. On the Great Lakes this spirit (or something very much like her) has been recorded in the Calumet Harbor area of Indiana, on Lake Michigan, which boasts a large Hispanic community. La Llorona, in the classic sense, is the ghost of a bereaved mother, driven to drown her own illegitimate children in a prominent area river or lake. Subsequently her phantom—clad in white with long black hair and claw-like fingernails—returns to search for them, often weeping as she does. "Weeping Woman" or "Crying Woman" is the English translated name. The Indiana stories claim that a Latina in white tries to hail taxis or hitchhike to get to Calumet Harbor. She then disappears while in the car, to the bafflement of the driver. The "White Lady" of DURAND EASTMAN PARK may well be yet another variation and elaboration of La Llorona.

LA VIELLE (See SUPERSTITIONS)

LADY ELGIN (See AUGUSTA)

LADY IN WHITE (See BELLE ISLE)

LAFAYETTE — Vague GHOST stories are associated with the Minnesota shore of Lake Superior, where the US Steel Corporation steamship *Lafayette* grounded and broke in half during an epic storm. The savage storm of November 28, 1905, is accounted by some to be one of the worst ever on the Great Lakes, with the temperature plummeting within minutes to twelve degrees below zero Fahrenheit and hurricane-force winds causing at least thirty shipwrecks. In nearby Duluth, some 40,000 citizens were said to have gathered at the lake's edge to watch the Coast Guard's desperate attempts to rescue the crew of the 6,900-ton *Mataafa*, which had lost her rudder and smashed against the city's piers (meanwhile a barge that the ship had been towing managed to safely weigh anchor and ride out the tempest). Half the *Mataafa*'s men froze to death in the stern section during the night before the waves and snow calmed enough to permit boarding. Given that tragedy, it seems curious that the revenant sailor associated with the storm alleged to hail from the wreck of the *Lafayette* instead. According to local legend, the apparition of a sailor from the ship is seen on the road near water. It may be just a coincidence—or just stoking wild rumors still further—that paranormal writer-researcher Loren Coleman has cited an unusual recurrence of the name "Lafayette" or its variations ("Fayetteville") in connection with bizarre circumstances and supernatural reports from across the United States, as though the name itself held some sort of sinister aspect.

LAKE ERIE MONSTER (See SOUTH BAY BESSIE)

LAKE LEELAUNA – Regional LAKE MONSTER reports about this body of water near Leland, Michigan, where the Leelauna Peninsula juts into Lake Michigan, center on a single 1910 incident. As the tale goes, a teenager named William Gauthier was fishing in a marshy, dammed-off portion of Lake Leelauna known as Carp Lake, when he attempted to tether his boat to what he took to be a large branch jutting out of the water from a submerged log. The "branch" opened a pair of eyes (apparently well above water level), stared back at the startled youth, and then swam away, proving itself a single great beast larger than Gauthier's rowboat. Though the creature — dubbed by some "Leelauna," the same name as the parent lake and the surrounding county — was supposedly seen on other occasions, when Scott Francis, intrepid author of the *Monster Spotter's Guide to North America*, personally investigated Lake Leelauna in recent years he found even local historians blissfully

A view of Silver Beach in Benton Harbor, Michigan, looking westward into the Lake Michigan Triangle.

ignorant of Leelauna's aquatic-monster traditions, though area INDIAN LEGENDS give the region as one of the roosts of the THUNDERBIRD. The idea of a mystery creature indistinguishable at a glance from dead logs and branches excites the more imaginative cryptozoologists because of the inference of some sort of evolutionary adaptive mutation, rather like "walking-stick" insects.

LAKE MICHIGAN TRIANGLE — Perhaps the most notorious of the TRIANGLES and VORTICES reported on the Great Lakes, this zone is said to occur within a triangular (some say rectangular) area marked by Luddington and Benton Harbor, Michigan, and Manitowoc, Wisconsin, with one vertice stretching out towards Chicago. LAKE MONSTER sightings have been recorded, as well as temporal anomalies, sensations of disorientation and dislocation, and things just not being quite 'right.'

The disappearance of the schooner *Thomas Hume* happened here during a Lake Michigan gale on May 21, 1891, while she was bound from Chicago to Muskegon, Michigan to pick up a load of lumber. Seven sailors, including Captain George C. Albrecht, were lost with the ship. No wreckage or bodies were ever found. A smaller-scale vanishing act that has become linked to the Lake Michigan Triangle in recent years is the disappearance of Captain George R. Doner, of the Great Lakes freighter *O.M. McFarland* on the night of April 28, 1937. While on a journey back from Erie, Pennsylvania after picking up 9,800 tons of coal, the ship made course westward through the lakes toward Port Washington, Wisconsin. Naturally, no "Lake Michigan Triangle" was delineated back then, but the ship was passing through these waters on the night of April 28, 1937—Doner's fifty-eighth birthday—when the captain simply disappeared. He had taken to his cabin, with instructions to be awakened as the ship approached port. About three hours later, the second mate dutifully went to Captain Doner's quarters to wake him, but found no one. Reportedly, the cabin door was still locked from the inside. The crew searched the ship, but never found a trace of Captain Doner. While it may have been a suicide, or conceivably the man leaving his room surreptitiously for a stroll and falling overboard (Doner had been diagnosed with a heart ailment), no one really knows. Proponents of the Lake Michigan Triangle prefer to add this mystery to their inventory of oddities.

Another disappearance was a Northwest Airlines DC-4 aircraft carrying fifty-five passengers and three crewmembers on June 23, 1950. Flight 2501 had departed from New York City for Minneapolis. The last radio contact put the aircraft at 3,500 feet over Battle Creek, Michigan, and about to change course to a northwesterly path over Lake Michigan due to bad weather near Chicago. After this, the plane disappeared and could not be reached by radio. The only clue turned up by a search was a Northwest Airlines blanket floating in the water. The codification of the "Triangle" in recent years has generated additional reports and anecdotes, including a vessel in a sailboat race in the 1970s suddenly draped in an anomalous, cold, dense fog, wind billowing in two directions at once, rotating the boat around while the crew lapsed into a sort of temporary trance state.

Reports of UFOS and USOS from the region include masses of witnesses on November 26, 1919, throughout southeastern Michigan, northern Indiana, northeastern Illinois, and the southeastern corner of Wisconsin...seeing brilliant lights in the sky and two large balls of fire falling into the lake, exploding on impact. Meteorites? When air controllers at Chicago's O'Hare Airport complained about numerous "ghost" images on their radar, causing some consternation in the control tower as planes seemed to be in imminent collision with objects that weren't there (not visibly, anyway), some Lake Michigan Triangle websites soberly noted the connection, even though glitch-ridden computer software was blamed. As Lake Michigan's air- and sea-lanes have been among the most heavily trafficked, no shortage of accidents, tragic circumstances, and unusual occurrences can be attributed to the "Triangle."

LAKE MONSTERS — Mysterious, large freshwater animals, unknown to science and resembling the general run of "sea serpent" reports from the world's oceans, have been reported in lakes and rivers of every continent except Antarctica. The most famous lake monster is, of course, 'Nessie,' the elusive denizen of Loch Ness in northern Scotland. Lake monsters are usually said to be generally serpentine (though with fins or flippers), varying from eight feet to eighty, and move through the water with an undulating motion, not unlike a giant seal. On rare occasions some witnesses report the creatures on land. In some instances, whiskers, hair, and horns are described. Some ride in the water with long, swanlike necks, offering a profile like that accorded by paleontologists to long-extinct plesiosaurs (this, however, would seem to be itself a misconception; recent research indicates the plesiosaur lacked the muscle and skeletal structure to raise its head in such a manner). Others seem more like descriptions of mammoth eels or magnified otters. Despite longstanding attempts to explain lake monsters as prehistoric survivors from the age of the dinosaurs, cryptozoologists have remarked on a "monster belt" or "monster latitudes," corresponding roughly between forty-five and sixty degrees north latitude, where such phenomena seems the most documented. These are bodies of water that for much of the year would seem too cold for the reptilian giants of the Jurassic and Cretaceous eras.

Most of the Great Lakes fall within these "monster latitudes," and parts of them have developed monster traditions, as have other, smaller lakes connected through the maze of Canadian river systems, well-stocked with Indian Legends about Naitaka, Mishipishu, and other marine menaces.

The sturgeon fish is an oft-cited suspect in Lake Monster sightings.

The Great Lakes are said to occupy favorable latitudes for the breeding of LAKE MONSTERS...

Monsters...

• **Ogopogo**: North America's most famous and oft-reported limnological monster, a creature (named, obscurely, after a British novelty song) supposedly dwelling in Lake Okanagan in western Canada; paranormal authority Loren Coleman has cited that area as the second place on the planet (after Loch Ness) for good monster spotting. An annual regatta celebrates Ogopogo.

• **Benzo**: Wisconsin's Lake Mendota was the stage of some rather spectacular encounters with a creature variously named "Benzo" or "Billy Dunn's sea serpent" (referring to an early witness); reports of this dragon-like thing were rampant from the 1860s, trailing off during the World War I years.

• **"Champ"**: More recently, multiple sightings and a few compelling (but far from conclusive) photo and video images have given credence to 'Champ,' a long-necked creature said to dwell in Lake Champlain, which connects tenuously to the St. Lawrence River. A resolution to protect Champ from harm or death was actually passed by the Vermont state government. "Champ Day" is celebrated in July (as the hotels and tourism industries of Scotland discovered, lake monsters can be a point of regional pride and profit).

• **"Memphre"**: A multi-humped animal between thirty and forty feet long is reported in Lake Memphremagog, a long finger-like mountain lake running south from Magog, Quebec, across the Canada/US border to Newport, Vermont.

• Other monster sightings tangential to the St. Lawrence's flow from the Great Lakes have happened at Muskrat Lake (home of '**Mussie**'), Lake Aylmer, and Lake Duchesme, all in Quebec. Mocking Lake, or Lake Pahenegamook, near the Maine/New Brunswick border, is habitat of the reptile-like '**Ponik**,' and Lake Utopia in New Brunswick is the domain of '**Old Ned**.'

Biologists who have studied lake monster reports from North America seriously have suggested that there is a possible prehistoric holdover breeding throughout the lake/river network. It is the 'zeuglodon,' or *basilosaurus*, an Eocene-era (about 37 million years ago) mammalian ancestor of the whale. Zeuglodon fossils indicate an elongated, snakelike body, up to seventy-five feet in length, with a fearsome mouth of sharp teeth and a possible dorsal fin.

More skeptical viewpoints suggest that wandering seals or other pinnipeds from time to time find their way from the ocean via the St. Lawrence and into communities where their unfamiliar presence triggers monster hysteria. Misidentification of freshwater lake sturgeon, a once-common fish and hunted nearly to extinction, with bony plates along its back, may also be responsible for monster reports, although five or six feet in length are standard for the North American sturgeon variety. Saltwater sturgeon can be more than twice that size, and Chippewa lore speaks of a tremendous sturgeon in Lake Superior able to capsize and sink vessels.

Archaic white-European lake monster accounts — most particularly those that speak of fearsome giant serpents with polka dots, bloodshot cyclopean eyes, and breathing fire and smoke — are certainly newspaper hoaxes, a pastime of the frontier press when there was a shortage of worthwhile news to print. Mentioned should be made of a minority opinion that the lake monster phenomena is occult/spiritual in nature...that these entities do not exist in the same material universe as the natural zoological order. This theory arises from the paradox of eyewitness reports combined with the frustrating absence (or disappearances) of carcasses or huge bones, and the failure of thoroughgoing scuba searches and systematic hunts, trawling, and drag-netting to find lasting physical traces of these seemingly huge creatures.

On the Great Lakes themselves, inland seas vast enough that any single one could dwarf Loch Ness, there would indeed seem enough room for something gigantic to hide. One of the oldest Great Lakes monster reports in print comes from Ontario, near the Niagara River. On August 5, 1829, the *Farmer's Journal* and *Welland Canal Intelligencer* wrote under the heading "Lake Serpent" that "children (from 10 to 14 years old) were a few days since playing on the lake shore, near the mouth of 10 Mile Creek, when suddenly appeared from the water a few feet where they were standing, a hideous water snake, or serpent, of prodigious dimensions." Their account described a body twenty to thirty feet in length and a head ten or fifteen inches in diameter with "warts" or "bunches" on it. It fled when the kids "gave the alarm." The report concludes that this was not the only time such a creature was sighted in Lake Ontario.

An August 1867 *Detroit Free Press* account describes in minute detail a Lake Michigan creature sighted by the crews of two ships, the *George W. Wood* and the *Sky Lark*, off Evanston, Illinois. A fisherman, Joseph Muhike (described as an "intelligent German"), later saw it a mile and a half off Chicago's Hyde Park. The monster, about twenty feet of which was visible, had whiskers or barbells on its snout, a ridged (sturgeon-like) back, front flippers or legs, and a long, possibly hair-covered tail. The fisherman actually heard it, too, a sort of "half puffing, like a heavy breath, and half an actual vocal sound, harsh and grating."

Around 1900 commercial fishermen in Lake Michigan off Milwaukee sighted a "ferocious looking beast." Soon afterwards boaters in the city's bay added their own monster reports, later compiled by the State Historical Society, of a large serpentine animal whose head was mistaken at first for a large, floating cask when the animal was floating at rest. It was also spotted from Milwaukee's Michigan Street Bridge, moving downstream on the Milwaukee River. The witness described a grayish-green serpent. In the Paint River, in Michigan's Upper Peninsula, two women counted six humps on a monster they saw in 1922.

Whitefish Point and Copper Harbor were the scenes of monster sightings in 1895. Some cryptozoologists attribute the relative frequency of sea-serpent encounters during the age of sail to the fact that the wind-propelled vessels used no engines, whose mechanical noise would doubtless repel sound-sensitive creatures. Yet in the summer of 1976, a resort owner in Cheboygan, Michigan, called the local sheriff to report two creatures, described as resembling catfish but approximately forty feet long, swimming in the Mackinac Straits of Lake Huron. The sheriff and a few deputies confirmed they saw something(s) perhaps thirty to forty feet long, which submerged when they tried to approach by canoe. More reports of serpentine monsters of similar length came in the next year from that area of Lake Huron. Other large creatures were seen (in some cases, two or more at once!) in the area of Kincardine, Ontario, near the southern Huron shore. A 1948 newspaper report from Georgian Bay described in rather tabloid-esque prose a sixty-foot green and purple scaly monster with horns that scared a summer excursion steamer's passengers and crew.

Of course, the prospect of hoaxes is never far from the rumors of lake monsters. A 1908 monster scare at Grand Traverse Bay was the result of public hysteria when a newspaper published a doctored photograph depicting a drawn-in monster on a view of the lake. In the early 1930s (the time period when the Loch Ness Monster splashed across international news headlines), a sham sea serpent made of thirty feet of wooden sections articulated together by wire, apparently meant to be towed by boat, was found washed ashore at Luddington, Michigan. That explained a recent spate of sightings.

(See also BABY ERIE, IGOPOGO, LAKE LEELAUNA, KINGSTIE, MERMAIDS, NETTLES LAKE, PRESSIE, and SOUTH BAY BESSIE)

LAKE SOLITUDE (See *GRIFFIN*)

LAMBTON — A tugboat outfitted as a Lake Superior lighthouse supply vessel, the *Lambton* and her crew of twenty-two men vanished in a storm in April 1922, with no bodies and only some minor wreckage found despite an exhaustive search. However she was said to have appeared again as a GHOST SHIP, notably in August of that same year, witnessed as a ship vanishing in the fog by Captain John McPherson, who was a passenger on another tugboat, the 124-foot *Reliance*. A Mrs. Charles Miron, wife of a lighthouse keeper, also claimed to have seen the resurrected *Lambton* through their binoculars. Captain McPherson, according to some accounts, interpreted the ship's manifestation as an OMEN of doom, and confided his feelings of foreboding to Mrs. Miron before boarding the *Reliance* once more, again as a passenger, on a late-season excursion to retrieve lumberjacks from camps along the Canadian shore. On December 15, the *Reliance* wrecked in freezing weather on rocky Lizard Island. McPherson and the others were left behind on the island as the crew braved the cold and angry Superior in a lifeboat to go for help on the mainland. When two additional tugs they summoned arrived on Lizard Island to pick up the rest of the survivors, McPherson was gone, along with two other men. Thinking the first expedition to the mainland had gone down in the pounding surf, the trio had launched the remaining lifeboat in desperation, only to be overwhelmed themselves. The wrecked lifeboats were found, but the bodies were not. Captain

McPherson's unease at seeing the *Lambton* again seemed to have been borne out.

'LEELAUNA' (see LAKE LEELAUNA)

LEMMY (See SOUTH BAY BESSIE)

LEWLAWALA (See MAID OF THE MIST)

LONG POINT — A finger of land on the north shore of Lake Erie, in Ontario, that has been a notorious shipwreck site since European navigation began. There are multitudinous tales of boats meeting their fates here among the sandbars and breakers, and heartrending accounts of sailors and passengers found frozen to death on the beach or in rigging after severe winter blows. Some reached the shore alive, but were unable to go on. Many had to be buried in the sand where they fell. A GHOST story about Long Point would be inevitable; what's surprising is that there are not more. The specter is supposed to be that of a sailor aboard a steamship caught in a gale in the 1880s. The captain had no choice but to launch a yawl that could get the crew to safety at Long Point, but in the ordeal of churning surf one of the men caught his head in a mechanism and was gruesomely decapitated, his body slumping into the yawl while his head tumbled into Lake Erie. Later his shipmates searched the shore for the missing head but never found it, and they reluctantly buried their crewmate without it. According to legend, on moonlit nights, the headless sailor still wanders the beaches of Long Point searching for the rest of his remains.

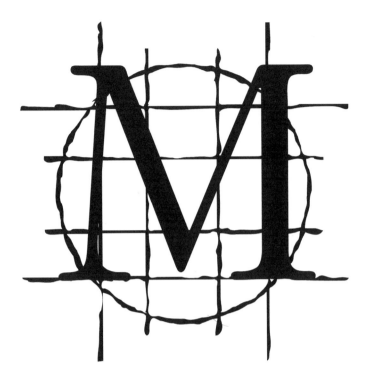

MACKINAC ISLAND — A much-cherished resort island off the coast of Michigan, named by the United States Congress the second National Park (after Yellowstone) in 1875, it has, throughout history, been a key stop at the juncture of Lakes Michigan, Huron, and Superior. Six miles square, the island is a sacred site in INDIAN LEGENDS and a burial ground whose full Ojibway name, "Michimilimackinac," means "big turtle," though one other translation is the slightly more mystical "Place of the Dancing Spirits." The popular English pronunciation is 'Mackinaw,' despite the spelling. A long and colorful heritage of European settlement, old Fort Mackinac, and a thoughtful plan to preserve the Victorian-style architecture and ambiance (thanks in no small part to a general ban on automobiles) has kept a nineteenth century milieu alive. The wooden white-pine Grand Hotel, erected in 1873, has been compared by many a travel writer to a wedding cake; it was a centerpiece of the location shoot for a popular film, the time-traveling romantic motion picture "Somewhere in Time," starring Christopher Reeve and Jane Seymour. In the warmer months devotees still flock to the island for pilgrimages to the backdrops and rent their own horse-drawn carriages. GHOSTS on this island would be expected. They include:

• The oldest ghost, arguably, is an **Indian maiden** who, according to legend, jumped to her death from a 145-foot limestone pillar on the western shore of the island; she was distraught that her suitor from a rival tribe had been slain by her father.

• The **apparition of a woman** was allegedly seen at Fort Mackinac as recently as 1985, tentatively identified as a widow of the fort's hospital steward, whose ship sank on the Lakes in 1887. The woman has not reappeared since a witness sprinkled holy water on the site of her last manifestation.

• **Phantom children** also supposedly haunt the fortifications, a ghostly piper perambulates on misty mornings, and a rifle-toting soldier still walks (and shots are still heard at a long-silent practice range). And the military post's cemetery is tenanted by the sound and occasionally the sight of a weeping woman.

• A **melancholy little girl** with long black hair, playing piano, weeping, and asking plaintively for her mother has been described as the resident haunt of not one but *two* century-old bed-and-breakfast inns, the Pine Cottage and Chateau Lorraine, both on Bogan Lane.

Pine Cottage—rather large as cottages go, with three floors and forty-two rooms—has a particularly bountiful supply of ghost tales. The place also purports to resound with phantom footsteps and doors opening and closing. In 1962 the new owner of the building opened a closet and was surprised by the apparition of a woman—visible only from the waist up—who rushed past him and out the window. She was popularly thought to be the victim of an unsolved 1942 murder. Items have gone missing, and Pine Cottage guests have claimed something pulls the bed sheets off them at night.

• The affectionate name of '**Harvey**' has been given to a ghost sighted at the Mission Point Resort: he is taken to be a lovelorn college student from long ago who committed suicide by leaping off a nearby cliff. It was a boyhood Harvey encounter that inspired local author Todd Clements to compile his authoritative volume *Haunts of Mackinac*.

• Small Point Cottage, built in 1882 along the foot of East Bluff, was moved to its present location after an adjacent sister house was torn down. The three-story house, then known as Old Turner Cottage, long had a haunted reputation when in 1971 teacher John Findley and his wife converted it to a bed-and-breakfast for the tourist season while spending part of year in their other home in Indiana.

The Findley would hear footsteps and unusual noises upstairs when nobody was there. A handyman also heard footsteps on the porch one winter, and not only did he find no person, but a fall of snow on the porch disclosed no prints either. Items would turn up missing, and doors would lock themselves (unless John Findley ordered the ghost to desist). Many believe the ghost to be that of a young girl who was forced to move away from the island, making good on her vow that she would one day return. Another suspect is a former owner, with a strong fondness for the house, who died within a month of moving away. Depending on which explanation is believed, the ghost is nicknamed either 'Aaron' or 'Mary.' The only sighting of an apparition was reported by two young boys staying at the cottage; they said that during the night a strange man had "sat in the air" by their bed and smiled down at them.

• A guest at the McNally Cottage Bed and Breakfast on Main Street reported a comforting visit from the late owner, **Shamus Mary McNally**, long after his death.

• St. Cloud Dormitory is supposedly haunted by a **noisy ghost**, especially room 33.

• And, perhaps inevitably, ghost rumors have attached themselves to the majestic Grand Hotel itself, though mostly they are inferred by the large quantity of Indian bones unearthed during the digging of the foundation.

While countless tourists have come to Mackinac for the local flavor, the delicious island fudge, and the tributes to "Somewhere in Time," there is a year-round (mortal) population of approximately six hundred. Island folklore claims that when a true inhabitant of Mackinac Island is about to die, a phantom nineteenth century funeral wagon pulled by black horses will perambulate through the streets as an OMEN. (See also SEBASTIAN and SUNKEN SISTERS)

MAID OF THE MIST — A heroine of native lore who has been embraced and robustly marketed by white enterprise in the tourist and honeymoon destination of Niagara Falls, lending her name to a popular excursion boat. Indigenous people invoked various INDIAN LEGENDS around the mighty waterfalls, and the divergent mythologies of Lewlawala, the "Maid of the Mist," wafts around them. In one account she is a widow grieving for her late husband; in another

Niagara Falls, where the "selling" of the MAID OF THE MIST as an authentic INDIAN LEGEND has led to recent controversy. *Courtesy of Charles Cassady, Sr.*

she is a girl trapped in an arranged marriage to a brave she hates; in yet another she is a human sacrifice by her own father to end a disease epidemic. In any event, she is a beautiful female doomed to go over the falls in a canoe. But He-No, the thunder demigod, is smitten with Lewlawala's beauty and rescues her. In some accounts, he makes a new home for her in a cave at the base of the falls, and Lewlawala eventually marries one of He-No's own sons. She is permitted to return to her tribe briefly to warn them when danger threatens. Lewlawala is said to appear in the swirling vapor rising from the cauldron of Horseshoe Falls in particular, on the Canadian side.

Author Ginger Strand, in her 2008 book *Inventing Niagara*, blasts the story of Lewlawala as having nothing to do with local Seneca traditions whatsoever. She concludes it was rather a lurid European-colonial invention, its trappings of doomed love, pagan sacrific and suicide consistent with nineteenth century novels and plays — written by whites — that titillated the public with the portrayal of Niagara's natives as savages. Possibly the only "authentic" portion of the legend concerns a side detail that Lewlawala's people are threatened by a treacherous, ever-growing two-headed snake, which Strand says, may symbolize the two-pronged pressure that the Seneca faced from the British and the French invaders. In 1996 the New York State American Indian Movement put pressure on the Maid of the Mist Corporation — operators of a fleet of tour boats bearing that name — to cease circulating the legend in their literature and audio tours, as none of the indigenous tribes and nations of the area ever practiced human sacrifice Nonetheless, Strand finds the Maid of the

Mist myths stubbornly, perhaps permanently, inculcated as part of Niagara's tourist-oriented culture.

MANABOZO ISLAND (See MICHIPICOTEN ISLAND)

MANITOU ISLANDS — Two islands in close proximity to each other in the northern region of Lake Michigan, both with notable legends of GHOSTS dating to the nineteenth century. Numerous shipwrecks occurred in the treacherous Manitou Straits, with many drowning deaths as a result. Disembodied voices from long ago call for help off South Manitou Island in particular, although the most infamous story of this nature concerns the earth, not the water. Allegedly in the 1800s a ship laden with German and Irish immigrants bound for Chicago suffered a cholera epidemic. To keep the scourge from spreading, the captain pulled in by night at South Manitou, secretly removed the passengers who had fallen victim and buried them in a mass, unmarked grave in the sand of the island's harbor—buried them whether they were dead or not. On foggy nights (or the anniversary of the crime, or both), the moans and wails of the stricken immigrants can still be heard. A more recent ghost reported is a small boy said to lurk around the wreckage of the *Francisco Morazon*, a steamer that grounded during a 1960 storm. The apparition, sighted numerous times by local park rangers, is taken to be an island farm boy who drowned while exploring the hulk.

At Sleeping Bear Dunes National Lakeshore, the South Manitou Lighthouse, first illuminated in 1840 and much remodeled and rebuilt (until it became one of the tallest lighthouses on the Great Lakes), carries the practically standard lighthouse-ghost legend of echoing footsteps and noises in the tower when nobody is there. It may be relevant that one of the keepers, Aaron Sheridan, drowned with his wife and child in March 1878, when their small boat capsized a mile and a half from shore.

Fewer ghost stories seem to afflict North Manitou Island, but those that do concern the 1877 United States Life-Saving Service Station, which has a counterpart on South Manitou, that once provided assistance to the frequent shipping emergencies of the Manitou Passage. Now both stations are seasonal quarters for the National Park Service, and rangers have reported hearing footsteps and, in the case of one female ranger, voices in the buildings, when she believed herself alone.

MANITOULIN ISLAND — The largest lake island in the world, Manitoulin is a scenic island on Lake Huron's North Channel, seventy-five miles long, and very irregular in shape, with hilly peaks rising 1,175 feet. It forms a principle demarcation between Lake Huron and Georgian Bay and supports several communities. The south banks of Manitoulin are particularly treacherous shipping lanes, and while there has been mild talk of a TRIANGLE at work, no paranormal forces are required to explain the estimated three hundred to four hundred ships (and even a few planes) that have gone down here. In addition, Manitoulin is rumored to be connected to the historic disappearance of the *GRIFFIN*, the oldest of the Great Lakes GHOST SHIPS. According to local lore, a "spectral ship," or "burning boat," regularly manifests itself off the shore of Manitoulin near Providence Bay, when the proper conditions are met. Potential witnesses must stand on the site of an old lighthouse now no longer in existence and wait for the hour of 3 a.m. on a night with a full moon. Then a flaming shape, seemingly the outline of a schooner ablaze, will appear in the water. Accounts claim that crowds of up to forty people at once have beheld this specter.

One *ghost* story connected with Manitoulin Island dates back to the War of 1812 and has attained frequent currency. The British maintained a fort on Drummond Island and two soldiers deserted. The commander posted a $40 reward for the men, dead or alive. Some Indians heard of this and tracked the deserters to a lonely beach, where the two fugitives had set a campfire. The Indians crept up behind the soldiers and decapitated them both with their tomahawks, taking the heads back to the fort to claim their reward. The bodies were left by the fire. To this day, the legend maintains, the headless duo haunt the beach. Sometimes passing boats will see a bonfire, with the truncated figures warming themselves. The grisly tableau disappears when witnesses draw near.

To the northeast of the Manitoulin archipelago are two islands prominent in INDIAN LEGENDS: Great La Cloche and Birch. Great La Cloche Island holds the remnants of "Bell Rock," a mystic rock formation for the Ojibway in that it rang when tapped. Even the early French *voyageurs* thought its tones reminiscent of a church bell and named the island accordingly. Sometime the chiming of Bell Rock would be used by the Ojibways to rally warriors against incursions by their traditional enemy, the Iroquois. After one battle, it was said, the Iroquois took the island and tried to make the rock ring, but it was strangely unresponsive to their hammerings; within three days the invaders had all died from a strange skin disease, allowing the Ojibway to return. Sometime in the last one hundred years or so, Bell Rock was found split into three fragments. A prosaic explanation is that white laborers at a nearby mine committed the vandalism. More exotic narratives states that a Christian priest smited the rock with a blessing, or lightning struck the rock, and it broke apart, much as the Indian way of life had broken under European domination. One fragment of Bell Rock is still said to ring.

The smaller Birch Island is the location of Dreamer's Rock, a site sacred to the Ojibway tribe and a traditional location for young braves to attain their "vision quests." One such pilgrim was the great medicine man, Shawonoswe, who received the equivalent of the Ten Commandments there from the world's Creator, and who was shown a prophetic vision of the coming of white Europeans and the strife that lay ahead for his people. Even today, Dreamer's Rock is a site administered by the natives of the Whitefish River First Nation. (See also YEO ISLAND)

MARINE CITY — Lake Huron shipwreck, whose disaster was supposedly the site of a lingering SPOOK LIGHT that bobbed over the water off Harrisville, north of Saginaw Bay. A steamer built originally as a barge in 1866 and later converted to a side-wheeler, she carried freight and passengers out of Detroit and around Michigan's Lower Peninsula. She even participated in an aborted expedition to lay telegraph cable through the Straits of Mackinaw. On August 28, 1880, she somehow caught fire after departing Alcona. The ship burned fiercely, but rescuers (especially the tugboat *Vulcan*) heroically pulled off all but nine of the possibly 140 passengers and crew (the exact figure of those on board is uncertain). Nonetheless, there were fatalities. It was said as early as the year afterwards that every August at midnight a mysterious, lantern-like light could be seen hovering over the wreck, whose hulk was still visible above the waterline as late as the 1950s. The light would drift away if anyone rowed out to investigate.

MARQUETTE & BESSEMER NO. 2 — A GHOST SHIP that been dubbed "the Flying Dutchman of Lake Erie." The *Marquette & Bessemer No. 2* launched in 1905, a 338-foot long, steel-hulled car ferry—not for motorcars, but rather railroad cars...an entire trainload of them. She carried thirty-two "hoppers" of coal when she headed out of Conneaut Harbor, east of Cleveland, on December 7, 1909, her daily routine bound for Port Stanley, Ontario, undeterred by a fierce storm. Her crew of thirty-six men was under the command of Captain Robert McLeod. His brother John, also holding a rank of captain, was serving as first mate.

The ship never reached its destination, disappearing in the three-day winter storm that had shook the lake. It has been theorized that the *Marquette & Bessemer No. 2* came within a few miles of Port Stanley, but then turned back towards Conneaut, perhaps by the combination of storm and notoriously poor lighting at Port Stanley. Workers on a dock there reported hearing a distress signal at 1:30 a.m. and another freighter captain riding out the night at anchor thought he saw the black shape of the car ferry pass by. Plotting the exact course of the *Marquette & Bessemer No. 2*'s final hours is a frustrating confusion of sightings and alarm whistles.

Three days after the *Marquette & Bessemer No. 2* disappeared, a grim find was made about fifteen miles off Erie, Pennsylvania. It was one of the ship's lifeboats, badly damaged, with nine frozen crewmen aboard, some still in sitting positions. Curiously, most were not heavily garbed, in deadly frigid weather, and an empty suit of clothing suggested there had been a tenth man aboard. Moreover, money—accounts vary from a substantial fortune to insignificant sums—had been kept in the ship's safe; there was also said to be $32,000 in a leather briefcase that last-minute passenger Albert Weis, of Erie, was to deliver for a fishery deal in Port Stanley. One of the dead sailors in the lifeboat had brought with him a quantity of knives from the ship's galley. Why? To defend himself? Against what? Captain McLeod's body, found later in river ice, had what looked like stab wounds. Out of these ingredients and the tragic loss of all hands—dead men tell no tales—much speculation of a dark nature has arisen about what may have happened and whether some foul crime had transpired, or even if UFOS and USOS were involved, as the survivors needed knives to defend against *otherworldly forces*. OMENS and PROPHECIES of the approaching doom have also been recorded. One crewmember allegedly wrote a letter stating, without elaboration, that this run would be his last voyage. A watchman's sister in Erie suffered a nightmare about the ship's sinking.

One likely theory is that the railroad cars broke loose, possibly smashing through the stern, enabling Lake Erie's angry waters to swamp the vessel. Captain McLeod reportedly complained that the ship had a tendency to take on water and nearly foundered from waves washing over her earlier that year. Great Lakes historian Mark Bourrie reconstructed a criminal scenario out of the evidence, theorizing that the men in the lifeboat were ten mutineers, inspired by greed or fear of the storm or a combination of both, so desperate to make a dash for land that they slashed Captain McLeod to ribbons and then took their chances, only to freeze to death instead (one of them so maddened with the cold that he shed his garments and plunged naked into the water, leaving the nine behind). In a final touch of melodrama, legends now call the *Marquette & Bessemer No. 2* a phantom ship. There is the claim that the vessel has been seen on Lake Erie, even from the air, on clear days. The sunlight streams serenely through the ghost's hull.

It may be worth noting that the shipping company subsequently built another ferry that it also christened *Marquette & Bessemer No. 2* (this immediate recurrence of a name was quite untypical, with or without the superstitious taboos surrounding SHIP NAMES). Some confusion has arisen, particularly in identification of photos, about which ship was which. They did look similar to the untrained eye. Could this have inspired the rumors of a ghostly resurrection? The second *Marquette & Bessemer No. 2* spent a trouble-free career, ultimately becoming known as the *Lillian* when she was sent to the scrap yards in 1997.

Another offbeat anecdote is told in connection with the original *Marquette & Bessemer No. 2*. Both Captain Robert McLeod and his brother, the First Mate, Captain John McLeod, were brothers of a third seafaring man, Hugh McDonald McLeod, commander of a whaleback steamer. It was on a December 7 that the *Marquette & Bessemer No. 2* embarked on its final journey in the world of the living. The next April 7, Hugh was notified that his brother John had been found, in ice on the Niagara River. Not until October 7 was Robert's body found, off the treacherous Long Point. Four years later, it was another April 7 when Captain Hugh McLeod, towing a barge on Lake Huron, learned that the barge captain had washed overboard and died the day before. The date that Hugh McDonald McLeod retired was, in some parts of the world, December 7, 1941, the "Day of Infamy" of Japan's horrendous sneak attack on Pearl Harbor and the US entry in to the Second World War. A coincidence...all these unlucky sevens?

The whereabouts of the physical wreck of the luckless ship is a storied mystery; she fits the "ghost ship" bill indeed. Something that large, downed in an area presumed to be just ten fathoms in depth, probably eight miles northeast of the Ashtabula County shore, should be easy to locate. Nobody has announced a definitive find, though the suggestion has been advanced that she has been discovered but the covetous scuba explorers keep the secret to themselves. Lake Erie divers and authors Georgann and Michael Wachter pinpoint the wreck lying six miles off Port Glasgow on the Ontario side, seventy feet down.

MARYSBURGH VORTEX — Late twentieth century paranormal authors gave this name to a portion of eastern Lake Ontario, declaring it a danger zone to ships and planes. It's located east of Point Petre in the southern portion of Prince Edward County and extends, in an easterly direction, towards the mouth of the St. Lawrence River and north in the direction of Kingston, Ontario. It includes Wolfe Island, where the lake narrows into the Thousand Island region of the St. Lawrence River, and where Ontario's deepest reaches have been measured to be more than eight hundred feet. Newspaper reports of strange lights in the sky in this vicinity, reminiscent of UFOS and USOS go all the way back to 1915. One oft-cited case of weird nautical happenings here was the schooner *Bavaria* in May 1889. With a crew of eight aboard, a steamship was towing her, along with two other schooners, when a storm blew up and the towline broke. Later the *Bavaria* was found abandoned and run aground on a shallow shoal near Galloo Island. One lifeboat was missing and only a caged canary was on board, among other signs that the ship had been hastily vacated. None of the crew was ever found, though supposedly two of the *Bavaria*'s men were seen clinging to wreckage, in water too rough to approach. More recent, contradictory tellings of the story are of decidedly eerier embroidery. They claim that the two men were actually observed seated in a yawl motionless, as though paralyzed or in a trance, as they went into limbo, and that nothing in the *Bavaria* was amiss enough to warrant her being evacuated for any earthly reason. She was repaired and put back into service, and to this day, she is something of a Great Lakes *Mary Celeste*.

Shipwrecks in the vortex region account for more than two-thirds of all shipwrecks reported for Lake Ontario—though this is one of the heaviest of all Great Lakes shipping lanes—and most of the "mysterious" stories date to the late nineteenth century, before improvements in ship propulsion, radar, sonar, and navigation overcame the hazards of sail. Still, there are allegations that pernicious electrical failures struck the 10,000-ton Greek freighter, *Protostatis*, in September 1965, leading to her scrapping. Fires and malfunctions similarly tormented the freighter, *Star of Suez*, around the same time. The tug, *Frank E. Barnes*, chugged into a fogbank near the Ontario shore in 1915 and was never seen again. Planes supposedly gobbled up or sabotaged by the Marysburgh Vortex include a Canadian Armed Forces CF-100 jet interceptor, which vanished over the north shore of Lake Ontario in September 1960, and a CF-5 jet that abruptly slammed into the ground in August 1977, without the pilot ejecting or displaying any prior sign of trouble.

Perhaps the queerest tale told of the Marysburgh Vortex is that in 1804 Captain Charles Selleck, of the *Lady Murray*, reported a huge "monolith" submerged by Presque Isle Bay. It was about forty feet square and lay just three feet under the water's surface, surrounded on all sides by a plunge of fifty fathoms of depth. Allegedly many villagers took their boats out to the bay to see this unusual structure for themselves. Soon afterwards, the three-masted government schooner, *Speedy*, set out, filled with dignitaries and even a condemned prisoner (an Indian convicted of murder), headed for the newly-founded town of Newcastle. The ship sailed into a storm and never arrived. Searchers approached the area of the monolith, fearing the *Speedy* had collided with the obstruction—only to discover that it, too, was gone. The monolith had disappeared without a trace; even trawling the bottom failed to turn up the pile of debris that would have resulted had the enigmatic structure simply collapsed. (See also TRIANGLES and VORTICES)

MCCOY ISLANDS (See BIG MCCOY ISLAND)

MENAGERIE ISLAND LIGHTHOUSE (See ISLE ROYALE)

MERMAIDS — A Canadian magazine in 1824 reprinted a curious item from the previous century as a Great Lakes "mermaid" sighting, although the witness himself never used the word or assigned a gender to what he said he saw. The man, Venant St. Germain, swore before Montreal judges and in a signed affidavit that he spotted a humanoid aquatic creature in Lake Superior on the night of May 3, 1782. After sunset, at the south end of the Isle Pate, he and his companions saw "an animal in the water which appeared to him to have the upper part of its body, above the waist, formed exactly like that of a human being." He compared the size to a seven-year-old child and a very human face. "The eyes were extremely brilliant; the nose small but handsomely shaped; the mouth proportionate to the rest of the face; the complexion of a brownish hue."

An Indian woman with St. Germain dissuaded him from shooting or otherwise capturing the creature, which St. Germain said regarded him with fear and curiosity; his Indian woman companion said that it was a manifestation of the "god of the waters" and must not be molested. The Indian woman also predicted an approaching deadly storm tied to the creature's appearance and made camp on high ground. That night a three-day storm struck. St. Germain said that another *voyageur* had seen a similar creature swimming.

INDIAN LEGENDS, especially Ojibway tribal lore recorded by Jesuit missionaries along Lake Superior, discuss "Nibawnawbe," aquatic mermaid-like creatures with waist-length hair inhabiting the shore of MICHIPICOTEN ISLAND since ancient days. "Fishes in the form of a man" was the description recorded by Antoine Denis Raudot in his 1710 memoir concerning the different Indian Nations of North America. Supposedly the sight of one was an OMEN of a death imminent in the witness' family. There are further vague rumors that French fur traders saw a child-sized creature in their early circuits of Georgian Bay, off Lake Huron. In 1937 in Saginaw, Michigan, a fisherman reportedly beheld a manlike amphibious creature clamber up a riverbank, lean against a tree, and then plunge back into the water.

METEOR (See *PEWABIC* and *METEOR*)

MICHIGAN (See SUPERSTITIONS)

MICHIPICOTEN ISLAND — This Lake Superior island of seventy-one square miles is situated within the jurisdiction of Ontario, Canada. Dangerous to approach by boat and often shrouded in mists, it was the subject of numerous INDIAN LEGENDS set down by early European explorers and missionaries. Ojibway-Chippewa lore claimed the island, also called Manabozo Island, was an unfixed, floating island—a myth one Jesuit explained by the atmospheric characteristic of fog making it look further away at times from the vantage of the Pukaskwa shoreline. Many spirits dwelt on Michipicoten, the tribes said, and traveler Jonathan Carver, in an 1871 book, wrote of one chief's tale that a group of Chippewa braves, driven ashore on Michipicoten, found the sand to be heavy, shining, and yellow—literally gold. But when they attempted to take some away in their canoe...

> "A spirit of amazing size, according to their account sixty feet in height, strode into the water and commanded them to deliver back what they had taken away... Since that incident no Indian who has ever heard of it will venture near that haunted coast."

White men did establish mining settlements, shanty villages, and a small lighthouse here, and there has been recorded in the annals a legend of a nameless GHOST SHIP haunting the island. To see the phantom vessel would be an OMEN of the witness' impending death. (See also MERMAIDS)

MINCH (See SHIP NAMES)

MINNIE QUAY — (See QUAY HOUSE)

MISHI GINABIG and MISHIPISHU (See INDIAN LEGENDS)

MOJAVE (See *AUGUSTA* and *LADY ELGIN*)

MYRON (See JINXES and JONAHS)

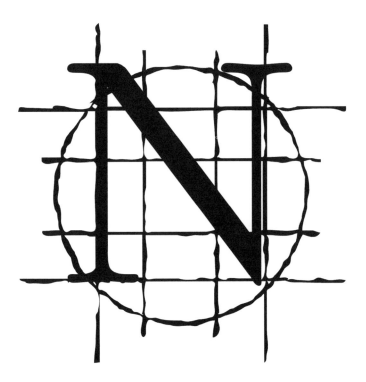

NAHANT — A 251-foot wooden steamer built as a bulk freighter in Detroit in 1873.

In late November 1897, she had moored at Escanaba, Michigan, to take on a cargo of iron ore, when a fire broke out. Two crewmen died in the blaze, which spread to a section of the dock. Local firefighters did their best to contain it and let the ruined *Nahant* burn out. A GHOST story is told about the wreck of the steamer, which was towed to a nearby beach and left for the winter. During a moonlit night in March, a local citizen claimed to have seen an "apparition" at large on the wreck. The figure seemed to go through the motions of digging in the charred hulk, as well as laughing insanely or crying out as if in pain. While circumstances suggest a lunatic or looter, the local newspaper was satisfied to put it down as a spook sighting.

NAITAKA (See INDIAN LEGENDS)

NEAL, CAPTAIN WALTER R. (See JINXES and JONAHS)

NELSON BLOOM (See *PEWABIC* and *METEOR*)

NETTLES LAKE — A lake off western Lake Erie, in Williams County; local traditions, sounding rather like wide-eyed campfire tales, speak vaguely of a tentacled LAKE MONSTER, preying on both humans and animals foolhardy enough to invade its swampy domain. Chris Woodyard, an Ohio-based collector of ghost stories and folklore, has also archived an obscure yarn that in the 1870s an old trapper named Sam Coon obsessively pursued a mystic treasure quest on the shores of Nettles Lake. Coon had somehow obtained an Indian tom-tom drum (bound in human skin, according to the tale), which he would beat to summon storms and the spirits of old chiefs, who told him of fortunes buried along the lake. But Coon contracted fever during one of his lonely expeditions and died ranting in his shack. The old man's one nephew showed up to search the hovel for any sign that Coon had indeed found the treasure, but there was only the drum — burst open, as though something had escaped from within. Though the shack has long since disappeared, the story concludes, the drum can still be heard pounding on hot summer days...just before storms.

NIAGARA-ON-THE-LAKE (See GHOSTS)

NORTH MANITOU ISLAND (See MANITOU ISLANDS)

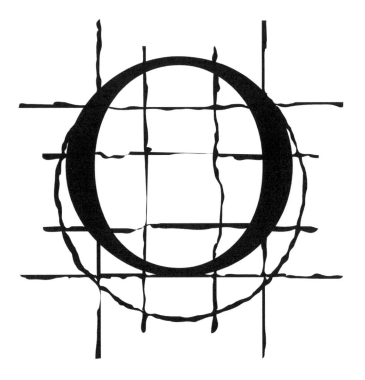

OLIVE JEANETTE — A four-masted schooner named for the two daughters of one of her owners, Charles J. Smith of Bay, City, Michigan, at 1,371 tons and 242 feet in length, she was a cargo-carrier in the Great Lakes age of sail. She also carried the reputation of being a JINX.

Used as a barge by the steamer *L.R. Doty*, she was in tow on Lake Michigan when a severe gale struck on October 24, 1898. The *L.R. Doty* foundered, but the *Olive Jeanette* escaped.

Then on September 1, 1905, she was being towed on Lake Superior by the 291-foot wooden steamer *Iosco*, both ships laden with iron ore, bound for Cleveland, when a monster storm hit that neither ship would survive. The lightkeeper at the Huron Island light said he witnessed the *Olive Jeanette* flying a distress signal in her final death throes—and the loss of the two vessels in the killer gale (that wrecked and damaged other ships, even at their moorings) littered the shores with debris and bodies—said to be in frightful condition. One victim apparently succeeded in crawling ashore...only to die from exhaustion, and when the body of the captain of the *Olive Jeanette* was discovered, it seemed he had tied himself to a spar in his final moments. Some of the dead turned up the following May, having spent the winter in ice. Of the twenty-seven lost, the captain of the *Iosco*, Nelson Gonyeau, was never found. There has been speculation his corpse was stolen by mainlanders who believed he was carrying the ship's reputed $800 in cash with him.

O.M. MCFARLAND (See LAKE MICHIGAN TRIANGLE)

OMENS and PROPHECIES — Portents of doom, ill fortune, or dangerous weather are frequent features of maritime lore—and the Great Lakes are no exception. Sometimes omens are anecdotal, taking the form of foreboding dreams or ghostly visitations, or visions that seem to predict a dire future. Sometimes they have a less individual character—like an invisible bell ringing or a GHOST SHIP riding the surf—perceptible (in theory) to multiple witnesses. Ojibway INDIAN LEGENDS even claim that a sighting of Mermaid-like creatures in Lake Superior foretold an approaching death in the witness' clan. More typical, however, are anecdotes such as the one concerning the sinking of the *Soo City* in November 1908. The Great Lakes steamship had been purchased with the intent to do a long-distance cargo run to New Orleans and back. The young ship's purser, James Anderson, of Montague, Michigan, even contracted with his community newspaper to mail regular bulletins to keep readers up-to-date on the epic voyage. Shortly after she passed Quebec, however, word ceased to come in about the steamer, with no other vessels reporting sight of her. A week after James' last message, his mother back in Montague reported a peculiar event. She thought she *heard* James and his brother Adolph "racketing about" in their upstairs bedroom, but nobody was there, as Adolph had left the house to trudge to the Post Office in case any more letters from James had been received. Shortly thereafter, debris from the *Soo City* washed up near Newfoundland. She had evidently fallen victim to a fierce Atlantic gale, leaving no survivors. What Mrs. Anderson heard was never explained.

On the Great Lakes themselves, disasters have left similar stories in their wake. They include:

The schooner *Volunteer* succumbed to an especially deadly Lake Huron storm in November 1869. Far away on land, the little granddaughter of the captain got out of bed at midnight and asked her family for a lantern because, she said, she had seen her grandfather standing by her bedside. The parents dismissed the girls' story as a mere nightmare, but subsequently learned that the ship—and Captain Disbrow—had gone down in the raging storm.

• A certain Benjamin Truedell, captain of the Great Lakes Life Saving Service in Grand Marais, Michigan, was said to be especially gifted with "second sight" and the ability to sense (though not prevent) an imminent shipwreck, as he did in a dream foretelling the 1892 end of the *Western Reserve*, one of the SUNKEN SISTERS.

• An ominous dream also preceded the end of the *Erie L. Hackley* in 1903. She was a steamer servicing the Green Bay port destinations of Lake Michigan. Roy Thorp, whose brother Ed was one of the ship's owners, had a vivid vision in his sleep of the *Erie L. Hackley* suddenly sinking in a gale. He said he nearly telephoned a warning to Ed, who had planned to be a passenger on the ship's next run out of Menominee, but relented. As it turned out, Ed Thorp decided himself not to embark, after seeing a threatening sky. So it was that on October 3 the steamer was hit by a squall that tore her topsides apart; eight men out of a crew of nineteen survived by clinging to part of the upper deck until morning, when a passing ship rescued them. Captain Joseph Vorous was one of the lost. When news of Roy Thorp's precognitive dream was made public, it served to fuel charges that the owners and their inner circle well realized and secretly feared that the ship was "unseaworthy"—something they staunchly denied.

• An alleged clairvoyant named Joseph A. Sadony demonstrated a remarkable psychic feat, if that's what it was. On September 25, 1930, he gazed out over a storm-tossed Lake Michigan from the eastern shore and told some onlookers that a commercial sailing vessel was in terrible trouble in the northwest, but that a steamer was on course to intervene. Some listeners pointed out that it couldn't be true. After all, schooners such as the one Sadony described were a thing of the remote past, but there, in fact, remained one holdover from the age of sail on the Great Lakes—*Our Son*, a fifty-five-year-old three-master. She was caught on the lake with a cargo of pulpwood for delivery at Muskegon and helpless in the tempest. She carried no radio and could only hang her distress flag upside down. Miraculously the steamship *William Nelson*, also on Lake Michigan, had altered her planned course in the storm, sighted *Our Son* outside of the accustomed shipping lanes, and was able to transmit an SOS as well as maneuver to the side of the battered schooner and offer sanctuary to the crew—more or less as Sadony had described.

Given the frequent perils of a seafarer's life, it would not be surprising for experienced seamen to develop sensitivity about menacing weather or potentially fatal sailing conditions, as these next wrecks show.

• Before the giant, 448-foot steel ore carrier *D.M. Clemson*, one of the largest ships on Lake Superior, went down in late November 1908, leaving no survivors, the widowed chief engineer, John J. McCoy, had telephoned his housekeeper—twice—to leave instructions about what to do with his children if disaster struck during the voyage.

• Frank Murray, a first mate on the 309-ton schooner *Plover*, in April 1871, suffered a nightmare in which he saw himself drowned. On the ship's early-season voyage, Murray disappeared during the night, apparently falling overboard unnoticed into the frigid Lake Huron while assisting another crewmember with the riggings. Six months later, while carrying 18,000 bushels of grain on Lake Superior, the *Plover* herself went down in an October gale; the crew of eight (including a new first mate) survived.

In contrast to the intuition of veteran lake men, we have stories from the tragedies of the *EASTLAND* disaster and the *WAUBUNO* of casual passengers suddenly overwhelmed with ominous dreams or intimations of impending doom.

(See also BLACK DOG OF LAKE ERIE, *CHICORA*, GHOSTS, *HUDSON*, *KALIYUGA*, *LAMBTON*, and OTTAWA DRUM)

ONNOINT — A monstrous serpent-like creature of INDIAN LEGEND among the Huron nation, who described it to Jesuit missionaries. Scholars believe the idea was imported from western tribes and their thunder gods. Onnoint was said to be a mammoth snake with a giant horn on its head, with which it could cleave through mountains, hills, and trees—or anything that would get in its way. Nobody had ever succeeded in subduing Onnoint or finding his lair, and to possess an alleged piece shed from Onnoint's horn was powerful medicine. Shamen who claimed to have such fragments would use them to embolden tribe warriors when going into battle.

ONTARIO — A Lake Ontario GHOST SHIP of some antiquity, being an eighty-six-foot long British sloop launched in 1780, outfitted to do battle, if necessary, with the rebellious American colonists. On Halloween night, suitably, in 1780, just months after her launching, while headed from Niagara to Oswego, she disappeared with all hands in a gale, taking at least seventy lives with her plus a substantial sum of gold and silver representing British payroll. No bodies were ever recovered, only clothing (chiefly hats), and despite a search for the money by treasure-seekers, only some hatch covers were ever found of the ship herself. Folklorish local color states that on stormy autumn nights the apparition of the old warship shows herself again on Ontario, still fighting the waves.

ONTONAGON LIGHTS — A regional occurrence of SPOOK LIGHTS said to happen each July 8 on Lake Superior, off Ontonagon, Michigan. Resembling flames burning out on the water, they supposedly marked the anniversary of at least two separate ship-fire disasters in the area. It may or may not be relevant that in July 1966, a local teacher reported a daylight sighting of a GHOST SHIP, a vintage two-masted schooner on the lake one morning when no ship known to be in the area matched that description.

ONTONAGON LIGHTHOUSE — A smallish, "schoolhouse-style" lighthouse built at the mouth of the Ontonagon River, where it empties into Lake Michigan on Michigan's Upper Peninsula. Its construction in 1866 replacing an earlier lighthouse on the site, its function was to serve as a beacon for the port's booming copper-mining traffic. This was a working lighthouse right up until 1963, and GHOST stories on the property seem to pay tribute to the well-remembered first keeper.

The spirit has been associated with Thomas Stripe, an Irishman who had worked both this lighthouse and the earlier one quite literally single-handedly. Stripe had lost an arm during an 1859 Independence Day celebration, when he saved a man's life by pushing him out of the way of a cannon. Despite his disability, Stripe lived with his family in the town of Otonagon, commuting to the Ontonagon Lighthouse (there was no keepers house) and servicing the facility alone. He used a special harness and hooks to clean the Fresnel lens from the outside and to haul the heavy oil can up the thirty-four-foot tower innumerable times to replenish the beacon's fuel tank. A legend in his own time, Stripe is said to have literally saved the whole community from starving during the winter of 1855, organizing a sled-dog expedition to retrieve food and supplies stuck in icebound ships on the lake. Stories claim that even after the loss of his arm he could still best any man in a fight. His term as keeper finally ended in 1883.

The Ontonagon Lighthouse is now the oldest building in the community and a national historic site. Guides and visitors have claimed to have found the relic oil can moved mysteriously from one floor to another and to have heard the distinctive clanking sound the can makes...as though someone were mounting the tower stairs with it and setting the can down at intervals to rest...*someone* with but one arm.

OSWEGO BREAKWATER LIGHTHOUSE — A Lake Ontario lighthouse built on a ten-foot concrete foundation rising up at the end of a break wall, the structure was completed in 1934. Despite its relatively recent vintage as a Great Lakes sentinel-beacon, the lighthouse is still said to be plagued with GHOSTS.

In 1942 six men drowned during a freak blizzard that trapped the lightkeeper in the building at the end of the breakwater for three days. Seven Guardsmen and a relief keeper set out to reach the light in a thirty-eight-foot picket boat, but a wave sent the boat smashing into the concrete foundation. Two Coast Guardsmen survived, but the replacement keeper and five of the would-be rescuers were never found again.

Subsequently strange events were recorded at the Oswego Breakwater Lighthouse. Light bulbs would be mysteriously unscrewed, furniture was found moved, voices and footsteps were heard when nobody seemed to be there, and the windows of the house would look ablaze with illumination, even when the place was abandoned and the windows boarded—as was the case after 1968, when the light was automated. In 1995 the Fresnel lens in the tower was removed and solar-powered flashing optics installed instead. The next year a commemorative service was held for the dead men and a monument erected in the City of Oswego. Whether that has satisfied the spirits or not is open to speculation.

OTTAWA DRUM — Name attached to a legendary OMEN of the lakes from Indian days, a booming male chant heard whenever a ship disappears. It has been said to have sounded first in conjunction with the disappearance of the *Griffin*.

OUR SON (See OMENS and PROPHECIES)

PEWABIC* and *METEOR — "If ever a ship was touched with the copper curse of the Chippewas, it was the *Pewabic*," wrote historian Dwight Boyer, of one of worst disasters in Lake Huron history, in which INDIAN LEGENDS figure predominantly, namely vague curses and maledictions said to strike those who covet and remove copper from islands and peninsulas of Upper Michigan, especially ISLE ROYALE. Certainly there can be an argument made that the *Pewabic* and her sister ship, the *Meteor*, qualify as JINX ships. They were 225-foot combination passenger steamship and cargo freighters driven by wooden propeller. The *Pewabic*'s elegant rosewood staterooms and stained-glass salons were complemented by 350 tons of copper (some sources report 500 tons) in ingots from the mines of Michigan's Keweenaw Peninsula, bound for Cleveland. She was on Lake Huron off Thunder Bay at dusk on August 9, 1865. There remains confusion over what exactly happened when she fatally crossed paths with her very own sister ship *Meteor*, heading for Sault Ste. Marie out of Detroit.

In fine weather, with clear visibility and no apparent malfunction, the *Meteor* simply smashed into the *Pewabic*'s port side, killing many of the passengers outright and sinking the copper ship near Alpena.

No doubt the toll would have been higher if not for the efforts of the *Meteor*'s captain, Thomas Wilson, to swing alongside and rescue the stricken of the slowly submerging *Pewabic*. But what exactly steered the two ships into each other remains a mystery. Great Lakes historian William Ratigan has suggested that one or both ships might have been trying to engage in a risky but not unheard-of maneuver (in the era before established shipping lanes) of passing so close to one another that mailbags and recent newspapers from port cities could be simply tossed from one deck to another. If so, nothing was spoken of it at the subsequent inquest. Death estimates are set

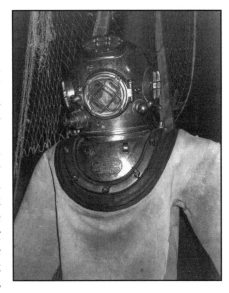

A deep-sea diving rig—the type used by salvagers in the dangerous treasure-hunt posed by the PEWABIC.

around 125. Talk of the *Pewabic* wreck was accompanied by rumors of $50,000 in gold on board in one strongbox, with possibly greater riches in a second safe, perhaps nonexistent (whatever the truth, the financial loss of the vessel did indeed ruin the shipping company that owned her). And, of course, all that copper.

Riches—real and imaginary—were sufficient to send treasure-hunters searching for the hulk 175 feet down. Several early divers, in ungainly, dangerous iron suits and clumsy air hoses, lost their lives on *Pewabic* expeditions prior to the wreck being pinpointed sitting on even keel on the bottom in 1897. In 1909 a New York syndicate whose owner had patented a newfangled diving outfit mounted a large-scale salvage operation that suffered numerous accidents and malfunctions and was forced to give up in October storms. Next a Chicago doctor, with a set of boxcar-sized submersible tanks, attempted to bring up the *Pewabic* whole, but failed, leaving his tanks to rust on the shore. In 1914 a diving bell sent down to the *Pewabic* flooded, killing the two occupants.

Finally, with the First World War driving the price of copper higher, a 1917 expedition by the Leavitt Deep Sea Diving Company succeeded in reaching the *Pewabic*, finding the staterooms strewn with skeletons of those who never left the boat, and bringing up between fifty-five and 150 tons of copper and numerous relics, including bottled beverages from 1865 that were still drinkable. A cash fortune was indeed found—in paper money that was long rotted. A 1974 salvage operation by Busch Oceanographic was even more thorough, and many *Pewabic* artifacts can be seen today at the Jesse Besser Museum in Alpena.

And what of the *Meteor*? Merely two days after the 1865 catastrophe, she caught fire and was scuttled in twelve feet of water with a cargo of lime. No lives were lost. Repaired, she sank again after striking a rock at Middle Bass Island in Lake Erie in 1871. In a spectacular 1873 incident off Detroit, she somehow caught fire while moored with a cargo of gunpowder. Towed away from the docks, the *Meteor* aspired to live up to her name as the gunpowder exploded, but the force of the blast was mostly directed upwards. One man died, but the ship herself was sound enough to be rebuilt and she was refashioned into a schooner-barge and renamed the *Nelson Bloom*. She was finally abandoned in 1925.

PHANTOM SHIPS (See GHOST SHIPS)

PINE COTTAGE (See MACKINAC ISLAND)

PIPE ISLAND LIGHTHOUSE — A lighthouse on St. Mary's River, a key waterway connecting Lake Huron with Lake Superior, the Pipe Island Lighthouse is an important navigational landmark along the passage. An octagonal thirty-three-foot-tall lantern tower and detached keeper's house was built here in 1888.

In 1937 an automated light on a steel skeleton extension relieved the old tower of its duties, and the Pipe Island Lighthouse passed through a succession of owners, becoming a hunting lodge, an outpost of the Nature Conservancy, and, in the twenty-first century, a vacation-rental property. Among the amenities is a GHOST legend that one of the old light keepers—tentatively identified as Norman Powel Hawkins—still keeps watch here. Tragic lore claims that he lost his son in a hunting accident and committed suicide. Later keepers reported seeing Norman in dripping oilskins standing in the tower doorway. Other manifestations include light bulbs found unscrewed, doors slamming of their own accord, and water faucets turning on.

PLOVER (See OMENS and PROPHECIES)

POINT AUX BARQUES LIGHTHOUSE — Site on the "thumb" of Michigan, on lower Lake Huron, of which some peculiar GHOST stories have recently been compiled by Great Lakes historians Frederick Stonehouse and Wes Oleszewski, the Point Aux Barques lighthouse and connected keeper's house of 1857 (superseding an earlier, shorter beacon erected on the same bluff in 1847) was retired a century later, in the 1950s. It was eventually added to the National Register of Historic Places and converted to a marine museum, with a caretaker couple traditionally in residence at the newer, detached keepers' quarters. A pair named Ray and Martha Janderewski took over the job of overseeing it in 1992, and their adult daughter Pamela is described as being plagued by unease about the eighty-nine-foot tall lighthouse.

She woke late one summer night in the older building and saw her dog staring fixedly at something outside her bedroom. Following its gaze down a stairway, Pamela found herself looking into the eyes of a woman apparently in her 30s, attired in an apron and old-fashioned dress and hairstyle. The woman turned and walked into the small hallway connecting the museum to the lighthouse and was not seen again. Pamela Janderewski found the "encounter" reassuring rather than spooky. Author Oleszewski, photographing the newer keepers' house for one of his books, took a set of pictures of the facade that seem to show the curtains of an upstairs bedroom window pulled aside and someone peering out...yet *nobody* was supposed to be inside at the time.

Near the lighthouse was a rescue station of the United States Life Saving Service, which once lost an entire boatload of men when their surfboat capsized in April 1879 during a rescue mission. Stonehouse logged personal testimony by a Lake Huron yachtsman that in the mid-1960s—also in April—he was sailing through a thick gray fog off Point Aux Barques when, dead ahead at about fifty yards, there loomed a white-painted rowing boat of somewhat peculiar design, with about eight men in it. All were rowing except the helmsman, who waved. The sailboat had to tack sharply to avoid a collision, and when the yachtsman looked back, the rowing boat was gone. Its side had borne writing, but he had not been able to read it. He soon realized that had his sailboat stayed on course she might have torn out her hull on a treacherous reef. "Did the long-vanished lifesaving crew return to save him from disaster?" wondered Stonehouse, who also posited a connection to the white-garbed guardian spirit 'Doc' at the 1966 sinking of the *DANIEL J. MORRELL*.

PORTE DES MORTES — A strait linking Lake Michigan and Green Bay, it's also known as Porte des Mortes, and the Anglicized translations of the French, the Door of Death, and Death's Door Strait. It's located between the northern tip of the peninsula of Door County, Wisconsin and the Potawatomi cluster of islands. The dire name derives from picaresque stories written down at the dawn of white settlement. Most variations go thusly: In the seventeenth century, two indigenous tribes, the Winnebago and Potawatomi, warred over territory here. Discovering a plan by the Potawatomi to attack their camp, the Winnebago lit false signal fires luring the enemy to a treacherous point on the shore, where the warriors could rain their arrows and axes on the canoes below, as the hapless Potawatomi were dashed against the rocks by stormy seas. When a Winnebago war party dispatched against the now-defenseless Potawatomi, the area struck the Indians as a literal 'door to death.'

There is also a somewhat more amusing alternate explanation—that the French gave the passage its name in a deliberate ruse to scare English traders out of utilizing it. As a navigational hazard, the stories told about Ponte des Mortes would do a French propagandist proud, as even today the Strait is said to be littered with wrecks caused by the many shoals—mostly schooners from the age of sail, who had to resort to Porte des Mortes before the more convenient and safer Sturgeon Bay Ship Canal was completed in 1878. The Detroit Island Passage to the north of Plum Island is still considered especially dangerous for all but the smallest boats. Some famous shipwrecks have been attributed to Porte des Mortes that actually occurred elsewhere, such as the *GRIFFIN*. The area is said to have set the stage for numerous visions of GHOST SHIPS, with one late sighting in 1940 by two couples in a small cruiser on a full moon night. Near Gills Rock they reported being lifted on a wave high enough to see a schooner rigged with lights in the distance. The archaic ship had vanished from view, however, the next time they crested a wave. It is true that ferries use (and continue to do so) the safer zones of the passage that run to the large Washington Island, but this, they claimed, was no ferry.

It attests to the power of words that in order to set a more appealing tone for the surrounding region, the name Death's Door County was eventually shortened to just 'Door County.'

PRESQUE ISLE NEW LIGHTHOUSE — Some GHOST stories are told about this Lake Huron lighthouse, built in 1870 near Alpena, Michigan. Its exceptional 113-foot tower is the tallest lighthouse beacon on the Great Lakes, but the fact that several other "Presque Isles" (from the French, meaning "near island") and attendant navigation lights have existed, folk gossip may have been mixed up and attributed to this structure (see next entry). The tale most often told here concerns a lighthouse keeper's wife who went insane because of loneliness and her husband's infidelities. Allegedly he imprisoned her in a cell or tunnel beneath the complex, or perhaps inside that looming tower itself (nineteen feet in diameter at the base, with 144 steps). Ultimately he murdered her, and her vengeful shrieks can be heard on windswept nights.

According to Great Lakes historian Frederick Stonehouse, the grown daughter of a Presque Isle Lighthouse keeper remembered a curious ritual from her childhood. The tower itself would seem to cry, or moan softly, and her father would put his hand on the wall and say, "Don't worry, we love you. We will care for you." This same informant said that during renovations to the tower structure a curious artifact (considering the reputation) turned up embedded in brickwork near its summit. It was a small gold engagement ring that one of the workmen kept for himself. The Presque Isle Lighthouse Historical Society now maintains the lighthouse, and visitors can climb the winding stairs to the summit and contemplate the lake, if they wish... *or perhaps the legends*.

PRESQUE ISLE OLD LIGHTHOUSE — A thirty-foot tall lighthouse on Lake Huron, lit with burning whale oil when the lantern first came to life in September 1840.

After the new PRESQUE ISLE LIGHTHOUSE went operational in 1870, the obsolete older lighthouse sat abandoned for some years before being auctioned to a local family, the Stebbinses, who proved to be lighthouse enthusiasts. Generations of the family gradually restored the relic, ultimately turning it into a unique museum and a site listed on the National Register of Historic Places. In modern times a GHOST story has lingered at the structure.

A retired couple named George and Lorraine Parris were hired as caretakers in the mid-1970s. In 1979, somehow, the lamp of the "Old Presque Isle Light" illuminated again at night. The errant beacon could have caused a navigational pileup, and steps were taken to remove the wiring and the gear mechanism so the odd accident could not happen again. Yet, in 1992, shortly after George Parris died, Lorraine Parris started seeing a glow in the tower (where the antique Fresnel lens had been permitted to remain). She rounded up friends and family who confirmed the phenomenon and ruled out reflections from car headlights or the floodlights shining on the building after dark. Through binoculars they also seemed to see a shadowy figure moving in the lamp room of the locked and empty lighthouse.

Subsequently there were attempts to extinguish the glow by hanging heavy curtains and tarps, even removing light bulbs, and changing the focus of the Fresnel lens. Yet witnesses still insisted they could see a luminescence. Some also reported hearing footsteps and experiencing strange feelings of dread. A little girl reportedly went up alone to the tower and then came down saying she had been speaking to a man in the lamp room. She identified him from a photograph—the late George Parris. Some others have theorized that the ghost is one of the original keepers. In the mid-1990s the Stebbins family sold the lighthouse and museum to the township, which continues to maintain it.

PRESSIE — Nickname given to an alleged variety of LAKE MONSTERS inhabiting the vicinity of Presque Isle River, in Lake Superior, off the Upper Michigan Peninsula. Sometimes linked to local Ojibway Indian Legends of "Mishipishu," a huge underwater lynx, the creature is described by white witnesses as serpentine, sometimes with whale-like tail flukes, a longish neck, a horse-like head, and about seventy-five feet in length. A purported habit of Pressie is to bask on the surface, its head very much appearing as a log; luckless herring gulls that land on the "log" are straightaway eaten. Key witness to Pressie is one Randy L. Braun, who claimed to have had a daylight sighting of the heads of two undulating creatures in 1977, weaving in and out of the boulders in the surf at the beach. He took a photograph that seems to show reptilian eyes glaring on the nearer object — or perhaps it's just sunlight sparkling on a wet boulder. A hunter also allegedly saw a buck in the water literally bitten in two by an unseen leviathan.

PUKASKWA — A region on the Canadian northern shore of Lake Ontario, where ancient Cairns and enigmatic rock pits have intrigued modern archaeologists. It lies within sight of MICHIPICOTEN ISLAND, and some INDIAN LEGENDS treat the area as a sacred site of great antiquity. Most prominent is one that states a brave abducted a chief's daughter here, but while making his escape he found her a burden, and so he slew the girl. Her spirit straightaway transformed into a white doe, and in this form, she haunts the Pukaskwa River gorges where she died. To see the ghostly white doe is an omen of certain death.

QUAY HOUSE — A house in Forester, an eastern Michigan resort and campground community north of Port Sanilac, garners most of its fame as the onetime residence of James Quay and his wife, Mary Ann, who had come to Forester from New England. Their house bears the year "1852" prominent on the facade, as well as the reputation of being haunted by a regionally famous GHOST — their daughter Minnie Quay.

According to legend, Minnie Quay, at age 14 or 15, fell in love with a Great Lakes sailor. Minnie's parents strongly disapproved and forbade her from seeing him again. In a much-retold refrain, Mary Ann Quay scolds that she would rather see Minnie dead than with the sailor. In the spring of 1876, the sailor and his ship (no names provided) both went down in a storm. Soon afterwards, the heartbroken Minnie was left home alone in charge of her little brother Charles. A popular folk-ballad describes what transpired:

'Twas on the twenty-sixth of April
Her parents went away.
Down by the side of Lake Huron
This fair one she did stray,
A-pondering on the dreadful scene
Which quickly must pass by,
For she had now determined
In a watery grave to lie.
She waved her hand to Forester
As if to say good-by;
Then quickly in Lake Huron
Her body it did lie.
Before anyone could render help;
Could lend a helping hand,
Her spirit it was borne away
Unto the Promised Land.

Did the teenage Minnie Quay die for love? Does the heartbroken girl still wave to the living from the depths of Lake Huron?

(Lyrics were obtained from the website www.traditionalmusic.co.uk/folk-song-lyrics/Minnie_Quay.html.)

Minnie is popularly said to have walked to the end of Forester's main pier to drown herself in full sight of some locals. The old pier no longer exists, though its pilings are visible. Minnie's parents buried her in the Forester Cemetery on the north end of town and, in their grief, sealed off her bedroom at Quay House.

Though the tragic ballad states, "Along the sandy shore/The voice of one poor Minnie Quay we'll never hear no more," area folklore claims that Minnie's spirit did indeed come back. The girl reputedly haunts the house, the beach, Forester Campgrounds, and the shoreline...weeping for the sailor she still cannot find.

The stories go on to say that Minnie has reappeared, bobbing in the waters of Lake Huron, beckoning to young female witnesses; the ominous interpretation is that she wishes others will join her in copycat suicides — perhaps she wants their company. At least one girl is said to have indeed killed herself after a sighting. The Quay family tombstone, listing Minnie's name, is often visited. Pilgrims cognizant of the tale of Minnie Quay tend to leave little gift-offerings (especially coins) in tribute to the tragic, lovelorn teenager.

RACINE (See SHIP NAMES)

RASPBERRY ISLAND LIGHTHOUSE — A lighthouse on one of the Apostle Islands of Lake Superior, it was opened in 1863 on a clay cliff on Raspberry Island's southwest side, by the city of Bayfield. It's a frequently visited tourist destination, easily reached, and has the beacon built into the white, two-story keeper's house. A ghost story goes along with the light. It is said that heavy footsteps can sometimes be heard on the stairway leading to the second-floor bedrooms.

The most detailed account of the legend claims it's the mournful tread of "Archie," a young lightkeeper's assistant shortly after the Civil War. The complicated light mechanism usually required an assistant to operate successfully, and Archie was allegedly an ardent, rejected suitor of the daughter of the owner of a local lumber mill. He had vain hopes that getting the job of assistant lightkeeper would render him a more eligible husband. While tending the light alone over Christmas, Archie simply vanished. Meanwhile the girl eloped with her true infatuation, a fearsome Civil War veteran—the implication being that the lovers had somehow taken the trouble to murder Archie and dispose of his body to seal their engagement. The Raspberry Island Lighthouse was retired from active service in the mid-twentieth century; its Fresnel lens on display at the Wisconsin State Historical Society Museum on Madeline Island.

REINDEER (See *ERIE BOARD OF TRADE*)

RELIANCE (See *LAMBTON*)

ROCKMAN — Translated name of Ki-chi-ki-wa-na, a Paul Bunyanesque figure of INDIAN LEGEND—the Huron Indian legends in particular. Born at Hudson Bay, he was so huge he could fling icebergs around as easily as Indians threw snowballs. The last of his race, he traveled south in search of other giants but found none. Some versions of the story describe him as a menacing character whose temper even irritated other gods and spirits that advised Ki-chi-ki-wa-na to obtain a wife. At Georgian Bay, the Rockman asked a comely Indian maiden he had long fancied to be his, but she responded that she was already betrothed to a tribal warrior. Furious, the Rockman heaved fistfuls of boulders into Lake Huron that became the many islands of Georgian Bay. Then he fell, either dead or in morose slumber, from his broken heart. An alternate version of the tale: he tripped on a fish and fell by the shore, and the impact shattered boulders that became many of the islands in the bay. The fall killed Ki-chi-ki-wa-na, and his body was discovered by the Hurons, who buried his giant corpse (as best they could) with heaps of rocks, reserving the largest and flattest for his gigantic head. This is presently known as Giants Tomb Island, in Georgian Bay near the entrance to Penetanguishene Bay.

In ancient times, tobacco and other offerings would be left for Ki-chi-ki-wa-na at the giant's tomb, but only in daylight hours. At night, it was feared, as his formidable spirit would be stirred. Belief in Ki-chi-ki-wa-na persisted well into the coming of the white man. A writer describes the Hurons as mistaking a blast of ship's horn as the grumblings of a disturbed Ki-chi-ki-wa-na.

ROCK OF AGES LIGHTHOUSE (See ISLE ROYALE)

ROGER BLAUGH — In recent years GHOST stories have been told about this 858-foot ore carrier, constructed at the

American Shipbuilding Company in Lorain, Ohio. In June 1971, with the ship nearly finished and a month away from a scheduled launch, a disastrous fire ignited in the engine room during the initial fueling of the vessel. Four workers lost their lives, but the boat, though damaged, was finished and put to work in service of the US Steel Corporation.

Minnesota writer Hugh Bishop has collected tales from crewmen about an on-board phantom—a disappearing man in the bowels of the ship. A night security guard supposedly heard disembodied footsteps, in one instance on the deck that was dusted with snow; yet no footprints were discerned by the watchman. Not long afterwards, when the *Blaugh* was laid up for the winter, a lone worker heard the electronic sound generated by the telephone receiver in the engine being picked up and replaced, again and again. But nobody was in the engine room.

ROLLING MUFF (See GROSSE ILE)

ROUSE SIMMONS — Numerous legends have accreted around the tragic 1912 loss of this vintage schooner in Lake Michigan. The *Rouse Simmons* has become known as "The Christmas Tree Ship," although many vessels in the late nineteenth century gained that name by ferrying a seasonal cargo of fir trees harvested from coastal Lake Superior and northern Lake Michigan. These trees were hauled to populous Chicago and Milwaukee to sell to the many German-immigrant families, who had brought the tradition of indoor Christmas trees with them from the Old World. Because of the late-November season for the Christmas tree trade, the cumbersome nature of the cargo, and the tendency by entrepreneurs to employ old, ill-kept craft for the trade, such Christmas tree ships often ran into trouble on the waves.

The *Rouse Simmons* was actually one of a number of schooners dedicated to miscellaneous odd jobs and cargo-loading chores operated by the Schuenemann dynasty, originally northern Wisconsin settlers who relocated to Chicago. One brother, August, drowned in December 1898, when the fir-laden schooner he commanded sank within sight of Chicago. The other brother, Hermann, persevered as a Christmas tree ship captain, offering trees at a lower rate than his competitors, despite the occasional loss of one of the aging, creaking ships. Still the arrival of an Scheunmann Christmas tree ship under full sail every year became something of a local institution. Elements of Chicago's homeless population would be hired briefly to help unload, and Captain Schuenemann earned a reputation as "Captain Santa" or "Christmas Tree Schuenemann" for his good works.

The *Rouse Simmons*, a three-master, was constructed in 1870 and was named in fact for the founder of the Simmons Mattress Company. Schuenemann leased her in 1910. He was one of the seventeen men aboard on November 26, 1912, when a storm struck the ship off Wisconsin during her return to Chicago. Rescue crews sighted the stricken schooner from a distance in a blizzard, but were unable to approach in their surfboat—and she disappeared with all hands, the Christmas trees washing ashore in poignant heaps. Within ten days, the sinking of the "Santa Claus Ship" made front-page news in Chicago. Months later messages in a bottle, written in Schuenemann's own hand, washed up on the beach off Sheboygan. It described the loss of two crewmen and a lifeboat in the storm, and leaks overwhelming the boat. "God help us," it concluded. For years afterwards local fishermen found submerged fir trees snagging their nets, and when on occasion an anonymous skull or partial skeleton was brought up as well, it was a reminder of the *Rouse Simmons*.

In 1924 Captain Schuenemann's own wallet was found intact. The Schuenemann widows and daughters kept the *Rouse Simmons'* memory alive by selling wreaths and trees from a street corner shop and lot in Chicago right up until 1932. In 1971 divers finally located the shipwreck off Two Rivers Point, 180 feet down. Fragments are on display in the Milwaukee Public Library.

Superstitious tales about the *Rouse Simmons* include an account that swarms of rats were seen fleeing the ship's hold before her departure from Chicago on her last voyage, a sure OMEN of bad luck, as was the upside-down horseshoe-shape of her plotted route on the map. Schuenemann was said to remark to relatives that the 1912 November Christmas tree voyage would be his last, although it's possible he was under pressure by his wife (and some shipping news columnists) to give up the hazardous trade. First Mate Charles Nelson, Schuenemann's business partner, made similar remarks about it being the last trip. The ship is said to have left Chicago with an unlucky crew population of thirteen (four more men came aboard with the trees at Thompson Harbor, near Manistique).

Finally, the growing legend of the Christmas Tree Ship has told of sightings of the *Rouse Simmons* as a literal GHOST SHIP, with the first newspaper reports dating as early as August 1917. Sightings of a seemingly derelict schooner led reporters to speculate whether a "caprice of nature" had served to somehow *float* the sunken *Rouse Simmons* on Lake Michigan, but no witness ever succeeded in coming within close approach of the resurrected Christmas Tree Ship. She is seen Christmas Eve and Christmas Day, as well as the fatal anniversary date of November 23. According to author Rochelle Pennington, who has written extensively about the *Rouse Simmons*:

> "Some say the ship appears most often on misty horizons at dusk, while others will tell you to look for the ship in the twilight mists of dawn. But most often, it is said, the ship will return in the same way she left...fighting her way through a violent gale."

Pennington states she personally met an eyewitness—a respected retired schoolteacher in Sheboygan—who claimed to have watched the *Rouse Simmons* phantom on two occasions.

A stage musical based on the *Rouse Simmons* has been produced, and with the turn of the twenty-first century, a new Great Lakes tradition around the holidays is to re-enact the landing of the Christmas Tree Ship, usually with a sturdy Coast Guard vessel as a stand-in, dispensing fir trees and charitable gifts. The practice is carried out in Chicago under the auspices of a Christmas Tree Ship Committee, and the event is combined with a public service memorializing Scheunmann and his crew and other lost Great Lakes sailors.

SACRED ROCK (See INDIAN LEGENDS)

SAGINAW RIVER REAR RANGE LIGHT — One of two beacons built at the west side of the mouth of the Saginaw River on Lake Huron in 1876. They superseded an older lighthouse in Saginaw Bay, which was later dismantled. The tower of the Rear Range Lighthouse is said to be haunted by the GHOST of an old keeper, who made his family vow upon his death to keep the tower illuminated forever after. Shortly after the Coast Guard took over the light in 1939, regular reports described the sound of heavy boots tramping on the circular iron staircase leading up the seventy-seven-foot tower. Invariably the tower would be empty when Coast Guardsmen investigated the sounds. In an oft-repeated account dated to 1962, one Guardsman on late watch in the building woke another when he heard the phantom footsteps, and both of them were able to corroborate the pounding footfalls. But when they at last entered the tower, the result was the same—nobody was there.

SCOURGE (See *HAMILTON* and *SCOURGE*)

SEA GULL (See SHIP NAMES)

SEAWEED CHARLIE — A GHOST on the shore of Lake Michigan, seen in and near Evanston's Calvary Cemetery, immediately north of Chicago. He is said to be the spirit of either a victim of a ship sinking or a plane crash. Some stories pin him down as a World War II aviator who ditched in the water during a flight over the lake. Others claim he is pilot Laverne Nabours, who died in a 1951 crash during a training exercise from Glenview Naval Air Station. The apparition is said to crawl out of the lake and stagger across Sheridan Road to get into the cemetery. Motorists who glimpse Seaweed Charlie take him for an incautious jogger—at first. Some fear that they have run him down... only to find no *body* there when they stop their vehicles and check. Two Columbia College students are said to have spotted the ghost in 1993 and described him as a tall, thin glowing figure in a long coat. Other rumors link the lurching ghost with victims of the *EASTLAND* disaster of 1915, or the earlier collision of the *AUGUSTA* and *LADY ELGIN*.

Yet another interpretation claims that the spirit is that of a Northwestern University student named Leighton Mount, who perished in a 1921 hazing ritual; Mount was tied to a Lake Michigan pier and left overnight, and he was found dead in the morning. It may be relevant—or just a linguistic coincidence—that a frequently unwelcome weed throughout lawns and gardens in Illinois and the Midwest is known as "creeping Charlie."

SEBASTIAN — A Lake Michigan GHOST folk-tradition of great antiquity, centered on MACKINAC ISLAND, dating to the colonial days of French dominance. The otherwise-nameless Sebastian was a hunter, who went off on a voyage across the Straits of Mackinac; engaged to be married, he assured his fiancée that he would return to her. Though he and his ship disappeared on the treacherous lake, the French hunter keeps his vow by sailing his one-man phantom ship through the Straits every seven years.

SEUL CHOIX LIGHTHOUSE — A late nineteenth century lighthouse overlooking Lake Michigan on a part of the Upper Peninsula, it was so named by early French trappers because it was the "seul choix," or only choice, accessible to land on the shore for some one hundred miles. It was similarly the only choice for locating the eighty-foot tower attached to the red brick keeper's house. Construction was completed in 1895, and the site is now a showcase attraction maintained by the historical society of the nearby town of Gulliver. In 1988, renovation efforts at the keeper's house by inmates of the Camp Manistique Prison led to the structure's now well-established GHOST tradition.

Members of the work team refused to enter an upstairs bedroom because of some nameless supernatural dread; they claimed to hear disembodied footsteps and hammering, and smell cigar smoke without an evident source. Other visitors to the bedroom reported seeing a man with bushy eyebrows, mustache, and beard reflected in the mirror—*but not present in the room*. He has been named 'William'—the name of several of the keepers who manned the light during its years of active service from 1892 to 1965—but some authorities have also claimed he may well be a ship's captain who was visiting his brother, the lightkeeper, when he fell sick and died in the upstairs bedroom.

The legend claims that William was born in Britain, and that table settings in the kitchen that are left untended in the American style, with the fork to the left of the plate, will be found later rearranged as per British custom, with the fork on the plate. The persnickety ghost has also been observed gazing out the windows or watching at a distance from the woods outside the lighthouse.

SHABAQUA TRIANGLE — An area west of Thunder Bay, on the Canadian side of Lake Superior, rumored in some circles to contain mysterious forces that interfere with the operation of boat, aircraft, and even snowmobile engines. On the evening of March 8, 2003, a bright object, tentatively identified as a meteor, fell in this area, fueling further excited talk of UFOS and USOS. (See also TRIANGLES and VORTICES)

SHELDRAKE — A GHOST TOWN village in Michigan's Upper Peninsula on Lake Superior, located about four miles north of a community called Paradise and sixty miles west of Sault Saint Marie, Sheldrake was once a lumber town of 1,500 residents that thrived for some forty years in the nineteenth century, until relentless tree cutting doomed the industry. Several disastrous fires wiped out the town, the last one in 1926, and most of the town's remaining occupants moved south and founded the village of Paradise. Only a few buildings remain in Sheldrake today, with a handful of year-round residents, though the scenic region attracts a larger crowd in the summer. Ghost stories mention an old sea captain who stands on the dock overlooking Whitefish Bay. He has a pipe and a cape, and is usually seen by approaching boats. As they near the shore, he fades away and disappears.

Several houses in the *ghost town* have also had paranormal occurrences. They include:

• **The Palmer House**: Said to have lights that appear in the windows when no one is present and window shades that often rise and fall as if by an unseen hand.

• **The Hopkins House** is also reportedly haunted, as a glowing phantom has been seen walking through the rooms at night.

• The apparition-in-residence at **the Smith House** is described as a former logger with a heavy beard and bib overalls; he's sometimes seen sitting on the furniture or standing in doorways.

• In **the Biehl House**, a number of witnesses have reported a woman in a blue veil. Disembodied voices are heard, pictures fall off the walls, and faucets turn on by themselves.

SHIP NAMES — Prominent maritime SUPERSTITIONS are associated with names by which ships are christened. Some Great Lakes historians have remarked that certain names seem to carry built-in notoriety, conferring the reputation of a JINX from the outset, including:

• *Oneida* was the name of several wrecks, four of which sank in Lake Erie alone.

• At least three vessels called *Queen of the Lakes* suffered wrecks or burned to the waterline.

• The name *Phoenix*, conjuring up images of infernos and mythical rebirth, lived up only to the former when a 350-ton passenger steamer by that name, filled with Dutch immigrants, burned in 1847 on Lake Michigan, killing between 190 to 250 people (entrepreneurs for years afterwards sold thousands of wooden clogs, which they falsely claimed to be actual mementos of the dead that had washed ashore).

Another *Phoenix*, a tugboat, burned on Lake Ontario in 1863. The next year a barge *Phoenix* sank in a Lake Erie squall, and another *Phoenix* tugboat would burn off Detroit.

Other names, singled out by Great Lakes writers Dwight Boyer and Frederick Stonehouse, to be bad luck are a veritable A to Z:

Ada and *Albany*; *Baltic*; *Calcutta* and *Comet*; *Dauntless* and *Dean Richmond*; *Emily* and *Evening Star*; *Friday*; *Java* and *Jennie Graham*; *Minch*; *Racine*; *Sea Gull*; and *Zephyr*.

(*'Dean Richmond' was the well-known president of the New York Central Railroad; the fourth doomed lakeboat to bear his name went down on a trip that started portentously enough on a Friday the 13th.*)

Other Ship Names' Curses

• Names with thirteen letters are especially baneful, and names with an abundance of the letter 'A' also meet with disfavor.

• Changing a ship's "given" name is also supposed to provoke bad luck — unless, paradoxically (and confusingly) you are changing the name of a bad-luck ship, in which case the correct name change can reverse the tides of ill fortune.

Vindication of the superstition seems to reside with the case of the 173-foot side-wheel steamer named *Comet*; built in 1845, it was considered especially accident-prone. After eleven were killed in an explosion aboard the *Comet* in Lake Ontario in 1851, she was heavily renovated and renamed *Mayflower*. Her subsequent service was reportedly free of mishap—until management decided to return the name *Comet*, whereupon the accidents resumed, culminating in an 1861 collision with a schooner near Nine Mile Point, sending the *Comet* to Ontario's floor.

A 269-foot car ferry built in 1906, the *Anne Arbor No. 4* was another "hoodoo" ship, frequently grounding and stranding in the shallows of Lake Michigan. She became "lucky" with a 1937 name change to *City of Cheboygan* and suffered no further serious mishaps, ending her career as a floating fish-processing factory before finally going to the scrap yard in 1974.

• Naming a ship after a bird (apparently even a mythical one, as in the case of the *Phoenix*) or ones drawn from American Indian culture can also bring on the hoodoo, according to old sailors.

Is any name absolutely safe? Not really, for if any given ship—adorned with any given name—meets with destruction, ships who happened to share the same or similar names might very well also be in for a rough time. (See also *ADMIRAL*)

SMALL POINT COTTAGE (See MACKINAC ISLAND)

SNAKE GODDESS OF BELLE ISLE (See BELLE ISLE)

SOO CITY (See OMENS and PROPHECIES)

SOPHIASBURG TRIANGLE — One of Lake Ontario's alleged TRIANGLES and VORTICES, located about ninety kilometers west of the Marysburgh Vortex, off the western end of Prince Edward County at the entrance to Presqu'isle Bay. This region supposedly exhibits a fluctuation in the earth's magnetic field that interferes with the normal functioning of compasses and makes it difficult to enter the safety of the bay during a storm or low visibility. Many ships have wrecked off the villages of Brighton and Cobourg, where deadly shoals are plentiful.

SOUTH AMERICA — A Lake Erie GHOST SHIP; it was a one hundred-ton, two-masted wooden schooner with a six-man crew, including Captain Sheldon Bradley. She disappeared in 1843 on Lake Erie with a cargo of salt. She had been bound from Buffalo for Toledo. Yet another vessel reported sighting the *South America* sailing in a thick fog four years later, and the phantom schooner has been reported on occasion after that.

SOUTH BASS ISLAND LIGHTHOUSE — A distinctive 1897 lighthouse that served as a beacon on western Lake Erie until 1962, it presents a fetching sight. Unlike other such lighthouses, the lantern tower was built right into the keeper's redbrick Queen Anne home, rather than standing free separately. Its homey appearance belies a tragic beginning that has helped nurture GHOST stories. The first lighthouse keeper was Harry H. Riley, who moved in with his new wife. The next summer, August 1898, they hired a caretaker named Samuel Anderson, an eccentric individual who lived in the basement, kept a collection of live snakes, and grew agitated over the possibility he might contract the dreaded smallpox contagion (both snakes and smallpox being common throughout the region). The story goes that not a month later, Samuel, drinking heavily, screamed—"God save them all!"—and jumped to his death off the lighthouse cliff. Was it a suicide? Or something else? Two days after Samuel's death, on September 2, 1898, Harry Riley was arrested in Sandusky, declared "hopelessly insane," and locked in an asylum in Toledo, where he later died. Mrs. Riley ran the lighthouse for another year before being relieved by a new keeper, who lasted on the job for eight years. His replacement, in turn, logged seventeen years in residence at the South Bass Island Lighthouse—until he fell to his death from the island cliffs as well, in 1925.

Several more keepers tended the South Bass Light, seemingly without incident, until its own retirement. A spindly metal tour with an automated light, maintained by the Coast Guard, now rises in the air in the back yard, and the South Bass Lighthouse itself became property of Ohio State

University as a research facility. Long off-limits to the public, the South Bass Lighthouse began giving tours to visitors in 2007. The ghost stories describe weird noises and a furtive, disappearing figure, possibly that of Anderson. Supposedly some of the staff refuse to spend the night—and the basement in particular has an atmosphere of foreboding.

SOUTH BAY BESSIE — The most "official" of various terms referring to what is perhaps the most famous of Great Lakes LAKE MONSTERS. Also known as "Lem" or "Lemmy," acronymically derived from Lake Erie Monster—and, in some archaic references, called the Great Snake of Lake Erie—the creature was recorded as being seen as early as 1793 by the sloop *Felicity*; its captain chanced to startle a giant serpent in the shallows of the Lake Erie Islands.

An article by nineteenth century science writer Constantine Samuel Rafinesque described a sighting from two years earlier, July 3, 1817, of a freshwater "huge serpent." Rafinesque equated the lake denizen matter-of-factly with the alleged sea serpents cruising the world's oceans. The Erie serpent, witnessed by a schooner three miles from shore, was between thirty-five and forty feet long, a foot in diameter, and dark brown or black. Rafinesque lamented that the report did not specify smooth skin or scales, surmised the animal a hitherto-undiscovered giant eel, and (as was a mania of his) suggested possible Latin scientific names. His classification was a bit presumptuous, as the "species" has gone through long periods of absence from the sight of man, punctuated by some fairly spectacular returns and shameless publicity stunts and newspaper hoaxes.

- In 1887 two brothers named Dusseu reported "a fish with arms" about twenty to thirty feet long, writhing on a beach west of Port Clinton, Ohio, apparently in pain.

- An 1889 newspaper from Sandusky quoted the fishermen as having seen the water monster at Kelleys Island.

- An 1892 report from Toledo claimed the captain and crew of the schooner *Madaline*, inbound from Buffalo, were amazed at a fifty-foot serpentine creature with fins about four feet in circumference, violently churning the water before coming to rest and allowing the mariners a good look at it.

"It was a terrible looking object. It had vicious, sparkling eyes and a large head," the report said.

- A Canadian report from 1896 describes a thirty-five-foot long serpent with eyes the size of silver dollars basking near shore, observed by four witnesses for all of forty-five minutes on a peaceful May dusk. One of the onlookers, a captain, threw rocks at the monster, which would lunge at the projectiles as if they were prey, exhibiting a doglike profile to its head.

- A Sandusky newspaper report from 1912 that a sea monster had burst up through the spring ice and made for shore at least had the chivalry to announce itself in the end as an April Fool's joke.

- In 1931 an *Associated Press* bulletin from Sandusky suggested Rafinesque's Latin classifications might at last be applied; fishermen had stunned and hauled ashore a twenty-foot long serpent with dark, alligator-like hide. "Serious" cryptozoological books and websites still refer to this remarkable specimen, generally ignoring that the men turned out to be hucksters connected with the carnival trade, who were trying to pass off a python snake as the "monster."

- A community newspaper, the *Ottawa County Beacon*, tallied "modern" sightings of the Great Snake from 1960 and 1969. The latter witness, at South Bass Island, said an underwater snake of indeterminate length and two feet in width, nosed up to within six feet of him.

The Great Snake re-emerged with spates of widely-publicized sightings in the 1980s and 90s—ironically, a period when industrial pollution in the lake made its viability as a habitat for many fish a dubious proposition.

A frightened boater in 1985 called the Coast Guard to report the monster churning the water aft of him. A woman witness had a similar feeling of terror when what she thought was an upturned

Incarnations of SOUTH BAY BESSIE—the LAKE MONSTER—on the Lake Erie shoreline in Ohio include a restaurant, sculpture, and a sandwich. A professional hockey team has also goes by the monster's name.

boat off Rye Beach in Huron resolved itself to be a large animal with a prominent grin on its face. Also in 1985 two Cleveland Coast Guardsman alleged a snakelike monster off a municipal beach.

In 1990 two Huron firefighters—one a retired Coast Guardsman— spied the monster as a humped, thirty-five-foot long shape, which they said was definitely not a log or a sea wall. A couple running a charter-boat business saw something very similar at Kelleys Island. A few years later, on a July evening at Huntington Beach, west of Cleveland, a beachful of witnesses saw a ridged back, estimated between twenty-five and fifty feet long, rise out of the water. One of those present later paged through volumes of animal life and decided it most resembled a gigantic sturgeon fish.

Most South Bay Bessie reports focus on the southwestern part of Lake Erie, along the Ohio coast of the Lake Erie Islands—admittedly, popular resort areas for pleasure boats, decadent parties, and tourists, where drinking and carousing synergize nicely with a fun and exploitable monster legend. Even the *Wall Street Journal* published an article on the community's zeal in capitalizing on the monster tradition. The name "South Bay Bessie," in fact, was selected in 1989 from among 115 entries submitted in a contest held by the *Ottawa County Beacon*. In November 1990, the Huron town council, with an eye to the publicity, passed a resolution designating themselves an official monster capture and control center. The Huron Lagoons marina owner garnered international publicity by having Lloyds of London underwrite a $102,700 reward for anyone able to catch South Bay Bessie (or any unknown aquatic animal at least 1,000 pounds and thirty feet long) alive and well. The reward went safely unclaimed, though a 'holding pen' was prepared (actually just a foot-deep pool to hold dredgings from a local marina).

Ohio State University oceanographer and zoologist Charles Herbendorf was duly consulted on possible feeding habits of a lake monster. Herbendorf was game enough to suggest his own Latin name for the beast, *Obscura eriensis huronii*, or "rarely seen, indigenous to waters of Huron." He indulged in a mental exercise that biologists and limnologists have played from time to time, calculating just how many theoretical, carnivorous 'monsters' a lake could hold given size, water volume, quantity of fish to feed upon, etc. He concluded Lake Erie had the capacity to support 175 creatures of thirty-five feet or so and 2,000 kilograms in weight.

Herbendorf's personal opinion was that South Bay Bessie was actually an illusion created by schools of the lake's plentiful carp, herded into serpentine strings by sandbars and shallows. Other possible suspects for the monster's identity include the sturgeon (though one witness to a multi-

humped apparition denied this vehemently), which were once so plentiful in the area that 1880s Sandusky earned the title of "Caviar Capital of the USA," and wild exaggerations of the common black water snake, which nest, breed, and sun in massive quantities around the Lake Erie Islands, to the chagrin of phobics. A Jet-Ski rider who claimed to have sighted a long, gray creature called it a "porpoise." Automatic cameras took positions at parts of Lake Erie, and monster-sized forms were allegedly recorded on fish-finding sonar and even by satellite photos (though the latter may well have been mud or marl traces left by boats in shallows).

In 1994 a Huron man erected a fanciful sculpture of South Bay Bessie on the Huron River, loops of snakelike dragon visible to drivers passing by on an interstate highway bridge (he subsequently added a baby South Bay Bessie trailing the "parent," but this was stolen).

By the twenty-first century the Lake Erie monster was quite famous indeed, even if the actual sightings had trailed off. A popular area

restaurant is named after Lemmy, there are monster souvenirs, and a Cleveland professional hockey team was christened the Lake Erie Monsters, with all the attendant exploitation of the image of a reptilian cranium protruding from the surface of the world's twelfth biggest freshwater lake. (See also ERIE BABY)

SOUTH MANITOU ISLAND LIGHTHOUSE (See MANITOU ISLANDS)

SPECTRAL SHIPS (See GHOST SHIPS)

SPEEDY (See MARYSBURGH VORTEX)

SPLIT ROCK LIGHTHOUSE — A 1910 lighthouse on Lake Superior built out of yellow brick and spectacularly perched on the edge of a 120-foot rock cliff in Minnesota. Decommissioned in 1969, the lighthouse is now operated as part of Split Rock State Park and is a popular tourist destination; very likely one of the most frequently visited of the Great Lakes beacons, attracting about 200,000 people annually, according to one tally. Perhaps inevitably, a few GHOST stories have arisen connected with Split Rock Lighthouse. It is said that a tourist in the 1980s forgot his wallet and, returning to the thirty-eight-foot tower, now locked, he saw a silent man attired in a vintage lightkeeper's uniform. Later none of the staff could identify the man in the uniform. Some versions of the tale have the apparition wordlessly handing the tourist the wallet, others have it just staring unresponsive, down from the heights of the tower. That guides at Split Rock occasionally wear period costumes makes a rational explanation likely. When the *EDMUND FITZGERALD* went on her last voyage out of Duluth Harbor in November 1975, she passed the Split Rock Lighthouse. Now on November 10 of each year the beacon is relit in a public ceremony memorializing the lost vessel and her crew.

SPOOK LIGHTS — Most popular name for a worldwide GHOST phenomenon (though some paranormalists have also suggested obscure connections to UFOS and USOS). Known in various languages and cultures (*irrlichtern* to the Germans, *lyktgubbe* to the Swedes), it amounts to a small, usually moving light or glow in the night, sometimes flame-like, sometimes more like an electric lantern at a distance. Observers who attempt to approach find the source of the light to be ever elusive, constantly receding. Science generally accords the classic "will-o'-wisp" an explanation as combusting pockets of methane or "phosphoresced hydrogen" escaping from layers of rotting vegetation, although the overselling of "swamp gas" as a rationale for UFO reports in particular made the topic something of a joke. The exact process by which this organic luminescence becomes concentrated and bright on a regular basis is still a puzzle.

Folklore, meanwhile, supplies ready answers. Many inland spook lights are said to be the restless ghosts of bygone railroad men killed on the tracks or the cyclopean beacon of an unfortunate motorcyclist of yesteryear who died in a gruesome accident. Distant and reflected automobile lights have been put forward to explain spook lights, although this does not account for reports of some lights appearing long before the invention of the motorcar. Legends from the French settlers of the Detroit area in the 1700s speak of the *feu follet*, or flickering lights, on the wetlands around GROSSE ILE that would attempt to lure unwary travelers to their doom in bogs.

From Weller's Beach on the Canadian side of eastern Lake Ontario come stories of strange moving lights, possibly men killed in the wreck of the schooner *Belle Sheridan*, lost there in a storm in November 1880. Or perhaps, as some storytellers insist, it's Louis Stonehouse, the mate of the schooner *Garibaldi*, which was walloped by an icy gale just ten days later. Some of the crew escaped via surfboat, while the rest held on to the rigging until help arrived the next day. Stonehouse refused to come out of his cabin and was found frozen solid; speculation that he had a large sum of money he refused to abandon rationalizes the Weller's Beach spook light as the miserly sailor still looking for his hoard (some stories claim Stonehouse appears in more substantial form by day as a frightful, ragged figure).

An 1876 newspaper report from Washington Island, in Green Bay, on Lake Michigan, described multiple sightings of white lights, about the size of "a basket" a quarter of a mile off, bobbing over the mouth of the harbor on Thursdays and Sundays. The spook lights, seen by most everyone on the island, visited in winter when the harbor iced over, but sometimes in the summer as well. The haunting, said the locals, dated back two years earlier: A fisherman named Halley suffered dementia after getting hit on the head by a neighbor—on a Sunday—and later the stricken Halley took his boat and a cohort out on the lake in a treacherous November storm which fatally sank them—on a Thursday.

In more recent days, there are claims of ghostly lights in private backyards and privately-owned beaches fronting Lake Erie in Bay Village, west of Cleveland. A psychic on the case rendered her opinion that these are the unhappy spirits of drowned shipwreck victims simply buried in the sand where they washed ashore—and this indeed was a standard practice during the age of sail on the Great Lakes, as harried rescue crews summarily interred waterlogged bodies in whatever dunes and shoreline ground was available. And oftentimes, neglected to exhume unclaimed corpses later. (See also: *MARINE CITY*, ONTONAGON LIGHTS)

ST. ALBINS — A GHOST SHIP steamer abandoned by her crew on January 30, 1881, when she seemed in imminent danger of sinking. In late February of that same year, fishermen began telling stories about a ghostly steamship apparently without a crew and no smoke coming from her stack off the Fox Islands. Was the *St. Albins* still afloat after all? A search of the lake that spring failed to find a trace of the lost ship. Some authors have filed the curiosity among the strange things allegedly happening in the LAKE MICHIGAN TRIANGLE.

ST. IGNACE LIGHTHOUSE (See TALBOT ISLAND)

ST. MARTIN ISLAND LIGHTHOUSE — A Lake Michigan lighthouse and fog signal built in 1904 to assist the shipping traffic into Green Bay, although some sources claim the beacon was not illuminated until the next year due to a delay in hiring a keeper, a certain Christian Christiansen. It's unclear whether Christiansen or a subsequent keeper is the prime figure in the GHOST legend extant.

  The story claims that one of the keepers who dwelt here with his family had children who were to take a rowboat to nearby Washington Island to attend school. In roiling waves, the boat capsized and the children were lost. Subsequently a SPOOK LIGHT would be seen on the shore, presumably the ghost of the keeper looking for his offspring with a lantern.

  There is an alternative version to the legend as well, claiming that one night the lamp in the tower failed to illuminate come nightfall and a schooner wrecked on the island shoals in stormy weather. Scrambling ashore, the crew saw a faint green light bobbing and followed it to the keeper's home. There they not only found refuge, but they also found the reason the beacon was dark—the lone keeper had recently died. The small green light that had guided them to safety was, presumably, his spirit. The light was automated in the 1940s and has had no keepers since.

STANNARD ROCK LIGHTHOUSE — Stannard Rock is an underwater mountain deep in Lake Superior that rises 1,000 feet to break the surface, about twenty-three miles from the MANITOU ISLANDS. Identified as a hazard to shipping as early as 1835 but not fixedly charted until decades later, the remote site was determined as the location for an ambitious lighthouse project in 1877. Using stone quarried from Kelleys Island, the prefabricated lighthouse was laboriously built on the rock, equipped with pumps, a pier, and a residence for staff who would be manning one of the loneliest of all Great Lakes beacons—one completely isolated by lake as far as the eye could see. Rising 110 feet above the water and sixty-two feet in diameter at its multi-level foundation, Stannard Rock Lighthouse became operational in 1883 to warn against the area's maze of reefs and shoals. It was frequently shrouded in fog and, in bad weather, pounded by waves that washed over the lantern tower. Staff nicknamed the place "stranded rock" because of the remoteness. Some Coast Guardsmen were so struck by the loneliness of the station that they suffered breakdowns or refused flatly to serve here. Still working as a key Lake Superior beacon and weather-reporting station, Stannard Rock Lighthouse has been added to the National Register of Historic Places.

GHOST stories about Stannard Rock circulated in the aftermath of a disaster and fatality at the tower on the night of June 18, 1961, as the light was being automated and, ironically, would no longer need a regular crew. An explosion in a boiler room ignited tons of stored gasoline and coal, causing an inferno in the tower that incinerated one man outright, injured another, and left the remaining three light-tenders scrambling out a galley window. Unable to re-enter the tower, they huddled on a ledge on the rock's north shore waiting for rescue, which came after two grueling days. Disturbingly, no ship had noticed the lamp being out until the Coast Guard buoy tender *Woodrush* passed Stannard Rock on her regular run. The fire in the tower was still burning when the *Woodrush* picked up the survivors. A cause of the explosion was never firmly determined. Automation of the light continued, and maintenance crews visiting Stannard Rock thereafter whispered feelings of dread, especially after dark.

In 1993 a four-man crew from the Coast Guard cutter *Sundew* used a small inflatable to arrive at the lighthouse for routine maintenance. Rough weather blew up, and the men decided via radio communication with the *Sundew* to remain at Stannard Rock overnight until the waves calmed. When plucked off the rock the next day, the quartet claimed that the tower had resounded during the night with running footsteps and an invisible force had tossed around a quantity of trash cans they had brought.

STE. CLAIRE — A 174-foot steamer built in 1910 as a pleasure vessel. The *Ste. Claire* and her older sister ship *Columbia* were "Bob-Lo Boats," launched for the expressed purpose of shuttling merrymakers back and forth to Bob-Lo Island, a resort and amusement park (its peculiar name an Anglicization of "bois blanc," or "white wood," for the dense beech-tree growth) that opened in 1898 on the Detroit River, near Windsor, Canada. In 1991, the propeller-driven excursion boats were retired, and the park closed in 1993.

The allegedly haunted steamer STE. CLAIRE.

GHOST stories about the *Ste. Claire* received currency after a husband-and-wife team of Clevelanders purchased the ship in 2003 and undertook a costly and prolonged restoration project to return the Bob-Lo Boat to her former glory. The husband had a brainstorm to turn the ninety-three-year-old boat into a floating "haunted attraction" in the meantime. This way part of the moored, inactive vessel could earn money during the Halloween season while tarps hung and tools banged away at other sections. In this fashion did the pretty *Ste. Claire* spend Octobers festooned with monstrous skeletons, fake spider webs, animatronics, hissing air hoses, and hired actors as "the Nautical Nightmare."

But there were *actual* ghost reports as well. A mysterious figure was reported (most often by the husband) hovering near concession stands or walking between rooms that used to be quarters when nobody else should have been aboard. There was a story of a young passenger en route to Bob-Lo Island who took a dare to jump into the water; he drowned. After the *Ste. Claire* moved from Toledo to a long-term anchorage on the Black River in Lorain, closer to its Cleveland owners, a paranormal-investigation group—wielding pendulums, dowsing rods, and other instruments—did an extensive tour of the steamer. They claimed to have made contact with "the energy of a young man" named Richard, a former waiter on the boat during its early years; he had died lonely and considered the steamer his only true home. Somewhat less affection was shown by the City of Lorain to the *Ste. Claire*. As repairs and restoration proceeded more slowly than expected, the town's daily newspaper editorialized that the ship had exceeded its lease agreement to remain on the Black River. In City Council, the complaints were that the vintage steamship was an "eyesore" and blocked views of the new condo projects going up along the waterway. There were even fears the owners would try to turn the *Ste. Claire* into a floating casino.

Ultimately the *Ste. Claire* was towed from the Black River to friendlier climes (and a new investor) in Detroit. Restoration continues, and no paranormal activity has been reported — although, with the Nautical Nightmare still a seasonal fundraiser, that may conceivably change.

STONEHOUSE, LOUIS (See SPOOK LIGHTS)

STRIPE, THOMAS (See ONTONAGON LIGHTHOUSE)

SUCCESS — Supremely ironic name of one of the most notorious vessels to sail the Great Lakes or anywhere else, for that matter.

A 135-foot, three-masted barkentine, the *Success* was built in 1840 in Moulmein, Burma, of sturdy teakwood, and was used for transporting immigrants to Australia. During that continent-colony's great gold rush, in 1852, the government of Victoria grappled with a shortage of prisons—the strong-backed laborers who might otherwise build them were off seeking their fortunes in the gold fields and outlaws such as Dan Morgan and Ned Kelly were becoming notorious. Authorities decided to utilize the *Success*, anchored in the port of Melbourne, and several other idle boats, as ersatz floating prisons, outfitted with cells and shackles. In 1869, after hosting both male and female convicts (Dan Morgan among them; he would later lead a prisoner uprising at one point), the *Success* switched from warehousing human beings to explosives and she served as a floating munitions dump at Sidney.

Her unearned notoriety began around the late 1880s. Alexander Phillips, the first of a series of new owners, purchased the schooner intending to turn the aging ship into a barge. He soon realized, with a steady stream of sightseers, that a market existed for those morbidly fascinated with the early years of Australian settlement—the forced colonization of the country by miserable boatloads of lawbreakers, debtors, and prisoners expelled from England in the late eighteenth century. Abandoning his barge scheme, Phillips decided to instead outfit the ship with wax dummies and make the *Success* into a floating chamber-of-horrors attraction, quite literally touring the world. Several decades were added falsely to her age, and the *Success* was promoted as a bloodstained, century-old survivor of that "First Fleet" of wretched convict-colonists.

"Floating Hell" was an appellation frequently applied to the barkentine and she was characterized as a literal *Ship of the Damned*. Instruments of gruesome punishment, torture, and execution took their place on and below deck, exhibited to the gawkers, even though the *Success* had never used such dire implements in her penal career. Some of the prisoners who had served sentences aboard her were actually enticed back with job offers to be guides. One is reported as having finally committed suicide. But sifting fact from hype about the *Success* is a challenge to historians, as its assorted impresarios played up the most lurid aspects they could imagine. Eventually, under new management, the "Convict Ship" came to North America—leaving England coincident with the maiden voyage of the *Titanic*. The state-of-the-art Cunard liner did not survive the journey over the Atlantic; the *Success* did, going up both the Atlantic and Pacific coasts, and Great Lakes, making periodic circuits. Paying customers could vicariously experience the cat o'nine tails, the flogging rack, and the iron maiden, and contests were held to see who could last longer in the "black hole" — the ship's windowless, solitary confinement.

Couples could be married on board, flaunting various SUPERSTITIONS, with black cats, mirror-breaking, and ceremonies in Cell Number 13 as part of the package. "Ancient, Famous, and Infamous" read the handbills from one of her Cleveland anchorages. Besides putting in for the Chicago World's Fair of 1933, the *Success* was also a guest at Sandusky's Cedar Point amusement park and the Great Lakes Exposition of 1936, as well as having regular engagements at Detroit, Sheboygan, Charlevoix, Saginaw, Port Huron, Mackinac Island, Benton Harbor, Kingston, and Albany—wherever tickets could be sold.

Eventually, perhaps inevitably, *real* GHOST stories became part of the allure. Non-English speaking Russians and FINNS were the preferred crew, partially on the basis that they would be ignorant of the ship's heritage and ghastly hauntings (either that or they could be paid less). Strange sounds were reported issuing from the hold, and an unearthly blue light shone from the dreaded solitary-confinement cell. Much of the crew refused to spend time below deck, preferring to bunk topside, and this was attributed to the miasma of evil settled into the infernal cells. Harry Van Stack, a lecturer on board the *Success* for twenty years, set down a number of ghost accounts on paper. Rich Norgard, a modern historian who has long researched the epic of the *Success*, judges that Van Stack's own religious background (he was born in the Transvaal, in white-colonized Africa) very likely predisposed him to notions of ghosts in perpetual torment. The *Success* was, after all, cited in sermons from the pulpit and in school-essay contests (which were, of course, thinly-veiled promotions sponsored by the owners to snag more visitors) as solid evidence in the supernatural war between Good and Evil, no less so than the gallows.

Ultimately, interest in the *Success* dwindled, and by the 1930s her reputation as the oldest ship afloat was no hyperbole but quite accurate. As the old teak timbers began to give out, her touring

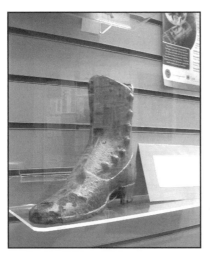

Artifacts recovered from the "Convict Ship" known as *SUCCESS* **are on public display at an Ohio library.**

days seemed fewer and fewer. In 1943, while being towed by a new owner, the old ship grounded on a Lake Erie sandbar. There she remained, at the mercy of ice and storms as well as human scavengers and vandals who stripped her of fixtures and furnishings. On July 4, 1946, somebody set fire to the Convict Ship. There has been speculation it was even an inside job, to get rid of a hulk that was more of a financial burden than anything else. She burned below the waterline as the fireworks lit up Sandusky's shore. Reporters had a field day describing how the many trapped souls must have soared, wailing and keening, out of her hold, freed from the "Floating Hell" by the cleansing flames.

The wreck, weighted down by a hull of marble for ballast, remains in easy diving waters about a mile from the Port Clinton beaches. Souvenirs of the *Success* are found throughout the communities of Lake Erie.

SUNKEN SISTERS — Popular nickname given to two late nineteenth century sister ships constructed by the Cleveland Shipbuilding Company, both the largest craft on the Great Lakes in their time—and both destined to be memorialized as GHOST SHIPS—after their brief careers ended dramatically, and mysteriously, in separate lakes...just sixty days apart.

The *Western Reserve* was a 310-foot, 2,392-ton iron-ore steamer launched in 1890, setting records for cargo hauls...as did the *William H. Gilcher*, which, at 318 feet long, was the largest boat ever built in Cleveland. But rumors claimed that the Bessemer-process steel used in their design could be dangerously brittle in rough surf. Captain Peter Minch of the *Western Reserve* was so certain of his ship that he took his extended family along with him on an August 1892 run out of Cleveland to pick up a load of ore at Two Harbors, Minnesota.

Many of the tales of the *Western Reserve*'s fate regard an OMEN that appeared in the form of a dream to one Benjamin Truedell, later to become captain of the Great Lakes Life Saving Service in Grand Marais, Michigan. In 1892, he was a junior crewman stationed at Deer Park, along

Lake Superior's "shipwreck coast." On the night of August 30, as a storm blew outside, he suffered a vivid nightmare. He dreamed that he was walking through the tempest outside and a well-dressed man approached him, gesturing out to the water and trying to say something, unintelligible, above the wind, rain, and waves. Then the man disappeared... Truedell awoke and told his comrades to expect news of a shipwreck. Although the night's watch passed uneventfully, at noon the next day the sole survivor of the *Western Reserve* staggered into the rescue station. He was wheelman Harry Steward, who told of disaster the previous night. The great ship broke in two in the gale, sinking in a matter of minutes about thirty-five miles from Deer Park. The *Western Reserve* had carried both a metal lifeboat and a wooden yawl, and only the latter, packed with nineteen people, managed to stay afloat in the rough water, with Steward steering. They attempted to hail a passing freighter for help, but the yawl carried no lights and went unheard in the storm. Soon after daybreak the yawl capsized, a mile off shore. For a time Steward and Captain Minch's young son stayed afloat, but the boy drowned before getting to the beach. The crew of the station, including Benjamin Truedell, combed the area for other possible survivors, but found only the bodies of the other twenty-five crew and civilian passengers of the *Western Reserve*. Truedell recognized one of the dead as the man from his dream—Captain Peter Minch.

Very little wreckage of the *Western Reserve* came ashore, and she found an afterlife in sailor lore as a phantom sighted at the height of storms. There are also stories of the spirits of the dead hovering around their graves in the sand, where some of the unclaimed bodies were summarily interred.

And what of the *Gilcher* ship? Only two months after the *Western Reserve*'s dramatic breakup and sinking, the *Gilcher* also disappeared. On October 28, she was passing through the Straits of Mackinaw and onto Lake Michigan, laden with more than 3,000 tons of coal and bound for Milwaukee, with a crew of twenty-two under Captain Lloyd H. Weeks. In theory the heavy cargo should have provided ballast and stability for the freighter. What exactly befell the *Gilcher* remains unknown. There was speculation that she collided with the wooden schooner *Ostrich*, which also failed to survive the storm, but the natural suspicion is that, like the *Western Reserve*, she fell apart from the pounding of the waves. Whatever happened, she never made port.

Her minimal wreckage washing ashore at North MANITOU ISLAND included lifeboat fastenings that had apparently been sliced away—clues of panic among a crew so desperate to escape they had no time to lower the lifeboats properly. But no bodies were found...just a handrail with a crewman's name "James Rider" and the time "9 PM." The *Gilcher* insurance write-off of $180,000 tallied the heaviest single loss incurred by underwriters on the lakes to date, according to local historian George Weeks, and the variety of Bessemer-process steel used in the two ships was considered no longer viable as shipbuilding material. The *Gilcher's* demise was more mysterious than the *Western Reserve's* due to the lack of any surviving witness or distress signals to tell the tale. In 1893 the wife of one of the missing crewman brought a psychic from Buffalo to determine the whereabouts of her husband, without success. More than one hundred years later, the site of her underwater wreck is equally unknown.

Reports of the *William H. Gilcher* as a Lake Michigan phantom declare that the coal steamer reappears when the fog rolls in by MACKINAC ISLAND. Manufacture of even more gigantic metal freighters would nonetheless continue, as would controversy over their seaworthiness and the wisdom of defying Poseidon's domain with such colossal, yet vulnerable titans as the *EDMUND FITZGERALD* and the *DANIEL J. MORRELL.*

SUPERSTITIONS — The essentially ancient nature of superstitious beliefs held by sailors and fishermen can be demonstrated in the still-common practice of referring to a ship as a "she." This was, in fact, a method by which seamen of Greco-Roman antiquity tried to curry favor with gods of the ocean—Neptune and Poseidon. By being considered female—and often given feminine names to accompany the common pronoun—boats were thus deigned virtual "brides" of the male marine deities, who would thus grant the ships and their crew protection and safe passage. That was the

Sailors in the 1800s observed maritime **SUPERSTITIONS**, echoes of which continue even today.

theory, anyway. When catastrophe did strike, however, superstitions down subsequent centuries supplied no shortage of explanations, in the form of taboos broken or lucky rituals neglected. They include:

• Setting sail on a Friday was considered dangerous, especially on the Great Lakes if the Friday happened to coincide with the beginning of the spring shipping season. Many a freshwater captain delayed casting off until a few minutes past midnight, when the date had safely crept into Saturday. If a sailor fell ill on a Friday, by the next Friday his fate would be clear, whether he was going to live or die.

• On Lake Superior November 11th—the eleventh day of the eleventh month—is considered especially lethal.

• Changing SHIP NAMES is traditionally bad luck—although, confounding historians, there are a few cases in Great Lakes annals when changing the name of a bad-luck ship seemed to take off a JINX.

• If a course is charted that takes the shape of an upside-down horseshoe on a map, then the "luck" theoretically falls out of it—and something awful could befall you on the route.

Not all superstitions are dire punishments; some dictate rituals that could win favor from the spirits. It was a custom among French traders and voyageurs, copied from the Indians, to offer little sacrifices (typically tobacco) to "La Vielle"—the "old lady of the wind"—for a safe, calm voyage or the assistance of a sturdy breeze at the back. Similarly, sailors might toss a handful of coins into the waves (off the stern) as an offering, either before the voyage or during it; this latter ritual intended to literally purchase a strong headwind. Other ways of inducing all-important wind during the age of sail included whistling or embedding a knife in the mainmast; coins—facing up, or else—could also be laid in the decks during construction, particularly at the base of the masts. Red wine should be used in a ship christening, not any other beverage (or water), and woe if the bottle fails to break, or if the ship does not leave the launch-ramp properly.

Old, beached shipwrecks are not to be broken up, but should be left respectfully where they grounded, to decay naturally. By the same token, salvaging equipment from a sunken ship (even though the practice was fairly routine) and putting it back into use is tempting an ill fortune for the new "host" vessel. This would especially have seemed the case for the nineteenth century steamer *WATER WITCH*. There is a story that two Lake Michigan fishermen netted a waterlogged old uniform from the notorious *CHICORA* and, recognizing it as coming from the alleged GHOST SHIP, immediately threw the find back.

Most of the superstitions held by Great Lakes mariners are mirrored by those of saltwater seamen, with a major exception: Despite the prevalence of ship's cats as rat-catchers on many vessels, and the concurrent veneration of a ship's cat as lucky, Great Lakes sailors decided that having felines aboard was bad luck. Lakemen suffering particularly troublesome journeys whilst hosting a cat said that the problems ended when the animal was put ashore.

Individual ships could have their own idiosyncratic superstitions and talismans. The *Michigan* was, in 1843, the first iron ship built for the United States Navy. Thousands of sailors trained aboard her during a long Great Lakes career (which, after 1905, saw her renamed *Wolverine*). Among her numerous distinctions was a lucky "wishing chair" in possession of the ship's steward. Acquired during a goodwill visit to Amherstburg, Ontario, in the 1890s, the chair supposedly held the power to grant the desires of those who sat in it. The steward allegedly filled five logbooks with testimonials from those who satisfied themselves in testing the chair's miraculous abilities.

According to waterfront gossip, one ship to be particularly punished by the fates for flaunting superstitious taboos was the 256-foot wooden steamer *F.A. Meyer*. New owners of the industrial hauler had changed her name from "*J. Emory Owen*," the name with which she had been christened after being built at Detroit in 1888. That partnership then fell into squabbling and suing each other over her earnings. In 1909 she sank in Lake Erie, damaged by ice floes. With her crew of eighteen taken aboard the steamer *Mapleton*, no lives were lost, but seamen remarked on the log of multiple transgressions:

- That August she had embarked on a run on a *Friday the thirteenth*

- She had at a time carried a crew of *thirteen*

- She was insured for $13,000, and on what would become her final voyage her cargo list included 1.3 million board feet of lumber.

- Some citations claim the date she went down was December 18, others that it was December 13.

(See also FINNS and OMENS and PROPHECIES)

SYRACUSE (See GHOSTS)

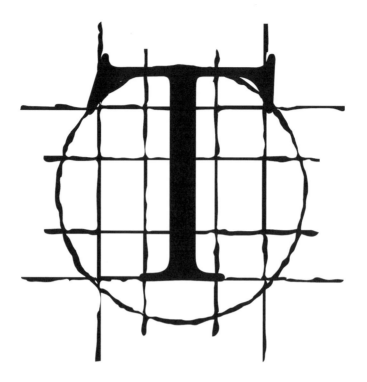

TALBOT ISLAND — A small island in Lake Superior, near the larger St. Ignace Island. GHOST stories told here relate to a now-vanished wooden lighthouse erected in 1867, the first Canadian lighthouse on Lake Superior. The St. Ignace Lighthouse earned the ominous nickname "lighthouse of doom" for the high mortality rate among keepers during its short span of service. The lighthouse was not easily accessible for re-supply over the winter, and the first keeper, a man named Perry, was supposed to close the lighthouse at the end of the shipping season and head for the nearest Hudson Bay Company outpost. Instead his body was found in the spring, washed ashore at Nipigon Bay. The second keeper, Thomas Lamphier, intended to spend the entire year on Talbot Island with his Indian wife in a new, well-provisioned house built alongside the lantern tower. However, during the first winter he fell ill and died. The island proved too rocky to permit burial, and Mrs. Lamphier spent several lonely months keeping watch over her husband's corpse to prevent animals from scavenging it, until in the spring a party of natives helped remove the dead man to Bowman Island to be interred in the sand. It is claimed that over the winter the wife's hair went from dark to snowy white because of her ordeal.

A third keeper died in circumstances similar to the first—of exhaustion and exposure after his attempt to get back to civilization for the winter. Now the Canadian government reconsidered the wisdom of maintaining the lonely sentinel on Talbot Island, and decided to abandon the lighthouse altogether. Though its lantern had been extinguished, the tower was still something of a landmark for fishermen, who found that they could also signal to each other by drumming on its walls with a stout stick. Those same fishermen, according to local lore, would sometimes see a white-haired phantom woman walking through the woods around Talbot Island—the grieving widow of Thomas Lamphier. Whether because of the stories or not, a few families of fishermen took it upon themselves to visit the Lamphier burial site on Bowman Island and maintain it.

TASHMOO (See JINXES and JONAHS)

T.G. JENKINS (See BLACK DOG OF LAKE ERIE)

THOMAS HUME (See LAKE MICHIGAN TRIANGLE)

THOMAS WILSON (See JINXES and JONAHS)

THREE-FINGERED REILLY — Colorful nickname given to a GHOST said to wander the shores near Whitefish Point, Lake Superior—a spot where so many shipwrecks have occurred that the Great Lakes Shipwreck Museum opened here in 1985 in the former keeper's quarters of the Whitefish Bay Lighthouse. Reilly was a boogeyman-like figure in the lore of the rescue teams and surfmen of the various stations along the coast. His origins date to November 13, 1919, when a 281-foot steamer, the *John Owen*, sank off Whitefish Point, leaving no survivors among the twenty-two aboard. One of the bodies, that of assistant engineer William Reilly, was found frozen on the shore the next March near Crisp's Point by a Coast Guardsman. The body had to be chopped out of the ice and was ultimately buried in a small cemetery adjoining the Coast Guard station. During the extraction, according to the mythology, an axe blow severed two of Reilly's fingers, leaving them behind on the beach. The phantom of Three-Fingered Reilly thus walks still, searching for his missing digits. Men on patrol blamed feelings of unease or the impression of being watched on Three-Fingered Reilly—or, possibly, on an indeterminate number of other ghosts said to be from local wrecks or earlier lifesaving crews.

THREE SISTERS — A much-discussed WEATHER ANOMALY wave phenomenon—associated with Lake Superior in particular—it was so feared by sailors it was given a name, if not the attributes of malevolent intelligence. The Three Sisters are a succession of three large waves that can literally batter a ship to pieces, like a series of hammer blows, or inundate the holds with tons and tons of water until the vessel can no longer stay afloat. The first two big waves come quickly, one after another. The third wave lags behind the first two, but is much larger...and it delivers the *coup de grace* that capsizes or sinks the boat. Even in modern times the Three Sisters were invoked to explain the loss of the *EDMUND FITZGERALD*.

THUNDER BAY ISLAND — A limestone island at Thunder Bay, east of Alpena, Michigan, it's the location of a lighthouse built in 1868 (replacing an earlier beacon), illuminating the treacherous passage of "Shipwreck Alley," which vessels had to navigate from lower Lake Huron to Lake Superior. During the 1930s and 40s, the lighthouse at Thunder Bay Island was reputedly haunted by the GHOST of a former keeper named Morgan. His spirit walks there because of his death many years ago. He died of loneliness in this desolate spot, a place so remote that the lighthouse was automated in 1983 with a solar-powered optic. The island is abandoned now—unless one places stock in the tales of Morgan's ghost still roaming the island's shoreline. A preservation society has been formed to protect and possibly refurbish the lighthouse.

THUNDERBIRD — A creature of INDIAN LEGENDS, it's of deep spiritual significance; in Ojibway belief, the giant thunderbirds, whose flapping wings produced thunderclaps and whose eyes shot out lightning bolts when they blinked, nested in the mountains overlooking Lake Superior. Mount McKay, near Thunder Bay on Lake Superior, was said to be an ancient roost of the thunderbird, and Indian tradition states that "nests" made of stone were seen in some parts of Ontario. According to one native tale, as recently as the nineteenth century, two boys dared to climb the forbidden mountain to see if the thunderbird really was there. At the top they discovered two hatchlings, big and hairy, whose eyes flashed with light as they blinked. It was enough to make the boys depart...quickly. Later the thunderbirds migrated away, to parts unknown. There has been a relatively recent vogue among cryptozoologists—those who give credence to the existence of LAKE MONSTERS and other unknown and legendary animals—to try to find factual evidence of the thunderbird as an unclassified, gigantic avian, perhaps even a prehistoric pterodactyl or other great winged reptile from the age of the dinosaurs. Scattered and bizarre reports of large-winged creatures, compared by witnesses to birds the size of small airplanes, or giant bats, or even airborne humanoids, have been much-publicized in the cryptozoological communities in inshore Wisconsin, Illinois, and Pennsylvania.

TOLEDO HARBOR LIGHTHOUSE (See GHOSTS)

TRIANGLES and VORTICES — In 1964 writer Vincent Gaddis coined the term "Bermuda Triangle" in sensational press articles and books alleging that weird events and inexplicable disappearances would befall both unwary ships and planes in a (very) roughly triangular area in the Atlantic, encompassing Bermuda, off-shore Florida, and the Caribbean islands. The name stuck when author Charles Berlitz published a smash bestseller by the same title in the 1970s.

Subsequent investigators have thoroughly debunked the idea of craft and people systematically vanishing there in unusual circumstances (basic fact checking into insurance records proved practically all of the mysterious disappearances could be attributed to localized squalls or storms—when the yarns weren't flat-out lies), and this mid-Atlantic route is actually, statistically, one of the safest in the world. No true mariner believes in the Bermuda Triangle or takes pains to avoid it. Nonetheless, the die was cast; millions of paperbacks sold, the popular imagination, hack Hollywood storytellers, and tabloid headlines had given a household name to the idea of a "triangle," not just in the Atlantic tropics but also in a similar "Devil's Sea" off Japan. And there have been propositions that some sort of "triangle"—maybe more than one—causes untold tragedies on the Great Lakes; the "logic" being that more sinkings and disappearances happen on the Great Lakes than in the dreaded Bermuda Triangle, therefore the paranormal forces at work are stronger.

The mechanisms by which such evil ship-swallowing zones work are none too clear. There are suggestions of high-tech energy sources from some long-sunken advanced civilization, maybe Atlantis, arbitrarily zapping and sinking vessels, for no real reason—and a few questionable (to put it mildly) theories have placed the legendary Atlantis, or something very much like it, in the Great Lakes area, roughly in or near Wisconsin. Author Ivan T. Sanderson proposed two mathematically progressing belts of "triangles" (actually oval-shaped spots) girdling the planet; one in the northern hemisphere, one in

Paranormal buffs maintain that mysterious TRIANGLES and VORTICES on the Great Lakes devour ships and aircraft without a trace…

the southern, adding up to a dozen "vile vortices." In these places, he theorized, rotating warm-water currents like the Gulf Stream could, via exotic physics, interface with cold fronts in the atmosphere and/or the planet's magnetic field to create a sort of variant on the "transporter beam" from "Star Trek"—a weird and dangerous anti-gravity force that could dematerialize a luckless craft or crew clear off the map.

Not one 'vortex' charted by Sanderson coincides with the Great Lakes. Nor are warm-water currents extant in these inland seas. Nonetheless, "triangles" have been claimed for eastern Lake Ontario and the air corridor stretching from northern New York State by Lake Ontario's southern shore, to Chicago on Lake Michigan. Allegedly a team of Canadian scientists in the 1950s discovered and studied "magnetic anomalies" or "magnetic declination" on Lake Ontario in particular, and their highly sensitive instruments measured variations in gravity near the shore of the lake. It has been suggested that within these areas, compasses and ship electronics could malfunction, and that the very nuclear binding forces that keep matter intact may be disrupted. These warps in the weave of space-time might not only trigger disappearances, but also inspire visions of GHOST SHIPS and other strange phenomena. Such vortices could even be intermittently operational gateways to other dimensions. Psychics and "dowsers" have claimed that clusters of energy and "ley lines" are active in the Great Lakes region, creating portals to other realms.

Yet another explanation—sometimes interwoven with the "vile vortex" theory in conspiratorial fashion—involves UFOS and USOS. It suggests aliens snatch the aircraft and boats for unknown nefarious purposes and perhaps use vortices in their furtive comings and goings. Legitimate science recognizes none of these theories, save one exception to extraterrestrial visitation: the magnetic anomalies be the consequence of an ancient meteorite impact dubbed by some geologists the "Charity Shoal" and leaving deposits of dense metal under Lake Ontario. Arguing against this idea is that field measurements supposedly found that these areas of gravitational flux were neither fixed in place nor permanent.

(See also: LAKE MICHIGAN TRIANGLE, MARYSBURGH VORTEX, SHABAQUA TRIANGLE, and SOPHIASBURG TRIANGLE)

TRIPP, AMOS (See COVE ISLAND LIGHT)

TROY (See JINXES and JONAHS)

UFOS and USOS — The acronym 'UFO' has been much misunderstood. Coined in 1956, it has two far lesser-known categories codified in early US Air Force reports: 'UAO' means Unidentified Aerial Object, denoting something of solidity and perhaps artificial construction, while 'UAP,' or Unidentified Aerial Phenomenon (or Unidentified Atmospheric Phenomenon) covers less tangible anomalies, such as lights, strange clouds, or haze. We'll come to 'USO' later.

The term 'UFO' and the slang-ish 'flying saucer' were inextricably associated on June 24, 1947, when a pilot named Kenneth Arnold reported spotting nine wingless, metallic-seeming disc- (or wedge-) shaped objects airborne near Mount Rainer in Washington State. It was much less known that not long afterwards Arnold, as one of the world's first "ufologists," went to Washington State to investigate a much odder sighting dated just a few days before his. A boater at Maury Island claimed to have watched several flying disks overhead come to the aid of another stricken disk, which discharged some sort of effluent (of which he was able to retrieve a sample). The saucer fleet then flew off. While little regarded at the time (one of the individuals publicizing the Maury Island event, a science-fiction publisher named Ray Palmer, was a notorious hoaxer, and Kenneth Arnold himself dismissed the account),

UFOs and USOs have been seen entering and emerging from inland lakes and rivers as well as the open ocean...

aspects of the story would come to dominate UFO lore in later years, especially the incidence of unidentified aerial phenomena over water.

After Arnold, a veritable saucer "fever," hyped by Cold War Hollywood B-movies and science-fiction tales about alien space invaders, took hold worldwide, spawning much speculation, as well as utter nonsense and outrageous hoaxes—and a good number of religious cults devoted to the coming of the "space brothers". Saucer 'aliens,' usually unseen, are now the space-age equivalent of the goblin, linked (by the true believers) to everything from power blackouts, shipwrecks/disappearances, and carcasses of diseased cattle dismembered by vandals and predators, to piles of industrial waste dumped illegally. The latter was likely the case with the "Les Ecureils iron mass": thousands of pounds of carbon and manganese steel found by the shale banks of the St. Lawrence River twenty miles from Quebec City in June 1960, which became a prize possession of the Ottawa Flying Saucer Club.

The romance of extraterrestrials largely ignores that 'UFO' can mean anything that is not a readily identifiable flying object (or IFO). Alternate, earthly explanations for UFO sightings have been proposed that run a colorful gamut: everything from luminous gas rising off rotting swamp vegetation to time-traveling visitors from humanity's own future, to psychological warfare and top-secret technologies being tested by foreign and domestic militaries; from roving electric-plasma fields generated by quartz crystals compressed by geological force ("earthquake lights"); and the sheer occult—some have noted the resemblance between "alien abductions" and Celtic "fairy lore," visitations to magical realms, and "changeling" human-fairy hybrids (who is to say that is less likely than flying saucers?); not to mention plain old frauds and stunts.

However, a maritime spin on the UFO phenomenon was proposed most prominently by scientist Ivan T. Sanderson, who noted that half of the UFO/UAO reports had a close proximity to oceans, lakes, reservoirs, canals, and rivers. While this would not seem statistically unusual, given that most of the Earth's surface is aqueous, Sanderson highlighted reports of UFOs sighted either plunging *into* or *out of* water, and produced the acronym USO (Unidentified Submarine Object) to suggest a form of highly advanced non-human craft capable of undersea maneuvers—as well as atmospheric ones—that regularly evaded naval vessels and aircraft searches. He suggested that either a space-going civilization had established a long-term base in the unexplored depths of the marine environment—or that highly intelligent life had evolved down there independently. The vast and maddening UFO dossier (part official government records and some from the more questionable sources of tabloid newspapers, "saucerphile" casebooks, catchpenny paperbacks, and newsletters) contains some interesting accounts of most unorthodox Great Lakes shipping. They include:

• In 1947, the year of the first great UFO craze, several independent witnesses in Milwaukee saw fireballs streaking over Lake Michigan (fireworks or flares would not be out of line as a possible explanation, as the date was July 5).

• In 1948 a nighttime fireball, described as weaving up and down, streaked over—*and possibly into*—Lake Ontario was seen from Bear Harbor Creek in New York State.

• In 1950 two Wisconsin policemen, in Whitefish Bay, beheld a red light over Lake Michigan; a Coast Guard ship sent to investigate found no UFO, but did meet, perhaps significantly, a US Navy research vessel on unspecified "maneuvers."

• In November 1951, a steamship captain and crew supposedly had a good enough look at an orange craft airborne over Lake Superior to say each side of it had six rows of two glowing "portholes."

• A TWA pilot told a UFO investigator of being "buzzed" by a flying saucer over Lake Michigan in August 1952, an encounter he refrained from reporting to the airline for fear of ridicule. That same month an Air Force radar base on Keweenaw Peninsula saw a formation of UFOs over Lake Superior.

• In December 1954, a Pennsylvania woman saw an object hovering on Lake Erie repeatedly over the course of a weekend; the second time she grabbed her binoculars in time and beheld a dome-shaped thing about the size of a tugboat with what appeared to be square windows. Multiple witnesses in Ashtabula, Ohio also sighted possibly the same or a different UFO that weekend.

• The year 1958 brought considerable action in the skies over the lakes. In April, hundreds of residents of Lorain County, Ohio, saw a fiery object "with horns" and trailing sparks over Lake Erie. In May, in Lake Huron, Canadian provincial police saw a "red flare" arc into the sky at about 1 a.m. and then plunge into the water off Grand Bend. In October, a fiery plane-like object appeared to crash into Lake Ontario, according to one witness from the New York side.

• Throughout the 1960s fiery nocturnal lights, sometimes flashing red, green, and white, were seen to plunge into the Great Lakes. Many may well have been meteorites, though some rather lurid reports from Canada actually describe saucer "occupants"—humanoid figures—walking around saucers or craft that hovered at an Ottawa reservoir and a flooded quarry between Lakes Erie and Ontario.

• In November 1967, guards on a tower at Kingston Penitentiary reportedly saw a slowly-rotating disk at about 8:45 p.m. shining a beam of light into the waters of Lake Ontario. A somewhat similar story is set weeks earlier, in September 1967, shortly after Ontario's Douglas Point nuclear power plant came online on the Canadian shore of Lake Huron, between Port Elgin and Kincardine. More than a dozen people (most if not all plant workers) saw a saucer-shaped machine on the afternoon of September 11 pass over the station and then hover a mile out over the lake. It seemed to drop something into the water. Over the next five nights, plant employees reported a similar craft returning and hovering near the station or the water. One witness reported that the disc gave off sparks. UFO commentators interpreted the behavior as the saucer leaving some sort of scanning/monitoring device concerned with the nuclear reactor and then returning to retrieve it, though the nearest military air base, Selfridge, claimed no unusual radar contacts.

• Another report of a UFO dogging an atomic power plant comes from the Pickering Nuclear Generating Plant in Pickering, Ontario. On New Year's Eve 1974 and again in February 1975, security personnel observed red, pulsating balls of light for about half an hour at a time. According to the UFO investigator who wrote the case down for the annals, reactor number three became disabled during both events.

• USAF jet interceptors scrambled in August 1975, when radar showed ten objects over Lake Superior moving southeast to northwest at 9,000 miles per hour; seven more seemed to appear near Duluth.

• Two Ohio police officers are said to be among the witnesses to a display of strange lights that came in shore from Lake Erie—and remained in view for about ninety minutes—over the town of Madison, on the night of November 4. The police radios ceased to work during the phenomenon, and a dispatcher who stepped outside also saw the lights.

• On November 11, 1975, F-106 interceptors took off from Selfridge Air Force Base in search of radar contacts corresponding with four bright objects in the predawn sky over Lake Huron. One—at least according to that paper of record, the *National Enquirer*—was viewed through binoculars by a Canadian police officer, who described it as a cylinder traveling in circles; despite these intruders being observed from the ground for a duration of three hours in the early morning, the jets failed to confirm the sightings. Just hours later, some where hundred miles to the west, the *EDMUND FITZGERALD* sank in Lake Superior—and some UFO enthusiasts have noted this, determined to tie the two incidents ominously together.

• In the pre-dawn hours of July 23, 1978, Coast Guard stations at Sturgeon Bay and Green Bay, as well as Luddington, Michigan, and Two Rivers, Minnesota, logged reports of a fast-moving UFO flying west over Lake Michigan; it was described by one as having red and white flashing lights. On successive weeks later the Green Bay Lighthouse and members of the Coast Guard saw a maneuvering light on two occasions.

• In fall 1993, several crewmen on watch on the Coast Guard cutter *Sundew* reported lights in the night sky near DEVIL'S ISLAND in Lake Superior. The array of lights was apparently attached to corners of a rotating body some three hundred to five hundred feet in length (or diameter). Radar did not register any aircraft or solid bodies present at the time.

• In July 2002, multiple observers at the mouth of the Thessalon River, on the Ontario shore of Lake Huron, reported white lights that seemed to be either just above or possibly even under the water before the strange display split into two groups; one UFO zooming off in the western sky, the rest going east.

It may be worth noting that Ohio State University astronomer Dr. Jay Allen Hynek, a longtime consultant and researcher into unknown aerial phenomena, was inclined to discount any reports of UFO/UAPs that amounted to lights in the sky. In his painstaking accounting of cases, baffled witnesses misinterpreted far too many ordinary things—planets, meteors, the moon, airplanes, and helicopters.

Still, author Hugh Cochrane claimed a Buffalo man (who refused to be named due to a family history of UFO sightings) was fishing on eastern shore of Lake Erie in daylight 1972 when a solid silver disc, thirty or forty feet across, erupted from the water less than three hundred feet from his boat. Another informant told a similar tale of fishing in the same area of Lake Erie in 1955 and seeing a bell-shaped object inside a brilliant light coming off the shore and flying over the waves, nearly colliding with his own boat. On a late afternoon in October 1961, three witnesses at Two Harbors, Michigan, claimed to see an object the size of an ore freighter skipping and bobbing on the Lake Superior waves before becoming airborne and disappearing towards the southeast. Canadians along the Great Lakes shores had some wild times with UFOs in the late 1960s and early 1970s, according to Cochrane, with multiple witnesses near Scarborough Bluffs on a June night in 1968, when three silent, luminous objects—one at least a hundred feet across—maneuvered at treetop level before disappearing over Lake Ontario. Someone made the curious observation that the glow of the UFOs did *not* shed light on nearby housetops and that commercial aircrafts at high altitude were in plain view during the display and bore no resemblance to the visitors.

Cleveland's newspaper carried the queer allegation that in March 1988, in the suburb of Eastlake, a couple saw a large "gun-metal gray" football-shaped object with lights, silent but with a rocking motion, descending out of the night sky toward the Lake Erie ice and shooting off smaller, triangular lighted objects. Reportedly Coast Guardsmen also witnessed this spectacle—and the fact that the lake ice seemed to crack and shift beneath the "parent" object. After one of the triangles noiselessly zipped close to the Coast Guardsmen's vehicle, the smaller UFOs rejoined the larger one, which then lifted off the lake surface and vanished.

Reporter Bob Pratt found the Minnesota shoreline of Lake Superior a veritable UFO hotspot, beginning with a 1975 mass sighting in which the witness spoke of swarming light balls in the sky moving rapidly and randomly, like popping corn. Sheriffs and other authorities saw the strange formation, and the fact that the report was filed on April 1—April Fool's Day—does not seem to have kept it from the UFO annals—or the fact that Pratt's newspaper was the *National Enquirer*.

Author Hugh Bishop has reported heavy UFO activity dogging ore trains moving through thinly populated forest regions by Taconite Bay, Two Harbors, and Silver Bay.

Lakes tangential to the Great Lakes that have left their names in the bulging and disorderly files of UFO lore include:

• Rice Lake, a fisherman's haven near Lake Ontario, into which a schoolteacher claimed to see a glowing object plunge on the night of September 12, 1969.

• Boshkung Lake, seventy-five miles north of Lake Ontario, is a site of annual regatta and picaresque resort living, and more—if the storytellers are to be believed. Cone- or bubble-shaped objects and pulsating lights dogged the lake in 1973 and 1974, and during the winter the dusk manifestations of cigar-shaped and "polliwog-shaped" flying things near and over the iced-over lake grew intense. So much so that irritated residents took their snowmobiles out and shot or threw snowballs at the invaders! The bullets could be heard pinging off hulls, went the story, adding that local authorities and Canadian defense officials took no notice of these queer complaints.

• On Washburn Island, a substantial landmass in Lake Scugog, between Lakes Ontario and Simcoe, a circular area of burned weeds, plus landing-gear marks—logically, a UFO resting point—turned up, coincident with mid-1970s reports of lights in the sky over Scugog, invariably moving southwest, towards Toronto and western Lake Ontario.

In the Great Lakes metropolis of Chicago, the J. Allen Hynek Center for UFO Studies (CUFO), on West Peterson Avenue, has studied the enigma since 1973. It maintains one of the world's largest collections of data on such aerial anomalies. Meanwhile, in the tradition of the late Ivan Sanderson, researcher Carl Feindt, via his website WaterUFO.net, continues enumerating cases of UFO-type phenomena that seems amphibious in nature. Consulted about the Great Lakes accounts, Feindt said that USO activity in this region, statistically, is neither more nor less intense than the rest of the planet's seas. "These guys go in and out of ponds, rivers — the Great Lakes are just another body of water." (See also: KINROSS INCIDENT and SPOOK LIGHTS)

USS COD (See *COD*)

VOLUNTEER (See OMENS and PROPHECIES)

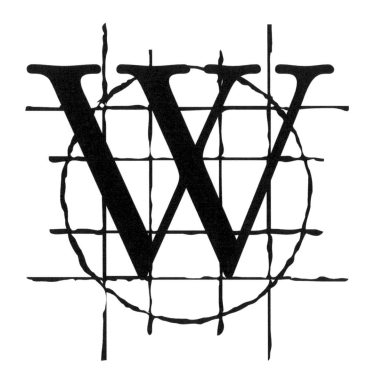

WALTER H. OADES (See JINXES and JONAHS)

WASHINGTON ISLAND (See SPOOK LIGHTS)

WATER WITCH — An alleged GHOST SHIP of Lake Huron, though there seems to be some confusion in the annals between this vessel and others with the same portentous name. This *Water Witch* was a 164-foot oak-planked steamer whose engine had actually been salvaged from a side-wheeler, the *Fashion*, a wreck in 1856. The *Water Witch*, built in 1861 in Newport, Michigan, enjoyed a reputation as the fastest ship on the lakes, as well as one of the best constructed. She was able to make eighteen knots on her borrowed steam heartbeat. But on November 11, 1863, as she headed from Chicago to Sarnia, Ontario, she was caught in a storm on Lake Huron. Another vessel, the bark *J.D. Norris*, also caught in the tempest, reported that the *Water Witch*, espied from a distance, seemed to be holding up well...then she simply disappeared from view in a twinkling. The twenty-eight aboard, including Captain George Ryder, were never seen again, though other ships subsequently reported a large field of floating debris in the vicinity. Conjecture has been that the ship's boiler suddenly, catastrophically exploded, either within or out of sight of the *J.D. Norris*.

Had, in fact, the men of the *Norris* been looking at a real ship—or an undead one? Allegedly the *Water Witch*, long lost, was sighted again several months later, by a steward emptying potato peelings off his own boat one night. He recognized the ship by her distinctive red smokestack and engine mounting as she passed by, silent and discomfortingly close, without lights or a warning whistle. Then the phantom dematerialized as he stared. Soon similar reports, or perhaps the same one retold, circulated through the maritime grapevine.

Great Lakes historian Wes Oleszewski has commented on a further bit of strangeness in the case: Captain George Ryder's brother was also a veteran steamship commander, Captain Redmond Ryder. A little more than ten years after the *Water Witch* disappeared or exploded, this Captain Ryder was steering the steamer *City of Detroit* in the same region of Saginaw Bay on December 3, 1873. A murderous winter storm assaulted that ship as well. This time the end was witnessed in detail by the stricken crew of another floundering vessel, the *Guiding Star*, who saw the crew of the sinking *City of Detroit* try to escape in lifeboats...only to be overwhelmed and drown in the icy Huron. The impression one gets, according to Oleszewski, is that sightings of the phantom *Water Witch* ceased coincident with the reunion of the Ryder brothers in death.

WAUBUNO — A 150-foot, two hundred-ton side-wheel steamer that regularly visited ports on Georgian Bay, Lake Huron, whose sinking in 1879 with all aboard lost (estimates vary to as many as thirty) is one of the region's most famous wrecks—and is associated with an OMEN.

Dr. and Mrs. W. H. Doupe, newlyweds from Mitchell, Ontario, were to sail on the *Waubuno* to their new home across the bay when Mrs. Doupe had a vivid nightmare of drowning in the icy November water. Her husband convinced her to keep their appointment nonetheless, even with a brewing snowstorm and choppy waves. The story goes that Mrs. Doupe confided her fears to other passengers in the port of Collingwood, and they, too, were inclined to cancel their own voyages, even though it was the ship's final scheduled run of the season. They were finally encouraged back on board by another traveler, a skeptical newspaper editor. The *Waubuno* embarked on its last journey at 4 a.m., November 22, 1879. Loggers on the Moon River heard her whistle...her last contact with the world of the living. Somewhere in the vicinity of Christian Island she sank in a gale, her life preservers and one lifeboat drifting ashore unused, judged evidence that disaster had overtaken the ship at deadly speed. Four months later an Indian found her overturned hull off Moose Point...a spot that soon became known as Wreck Island.

Besides the ominous dream, storytellers also cite the detail that not a single body was recovered after the *Waubuno* disaster—and that the ship's own name was supposedly the Algonquin word for 'sorcerer.' A woman garbed in antiquated clothing was reportedly seen by a boater at Wreck Island in the 1980s and has been assigned the identity of a GHOST off the *Waubuno*—perhaps even Mrs. Doupe herself. Equally noteworthy was the JINX that seemed to shadow the Georgian Bay Navigation Company, which owned the *Waubuno*. Their replacement ship, *Manitoulin*, suffered a fire that killed a few dozen people in May 1882. A ship put into service to replace the *Manitoulin*, the *Asia*, sank in Georgian Bay on September 14, 1882, killing 123 people.

WAUGOSHANCE SHOAL LIGHTHOUSE — A ruined lighthouse strikingly projecting above the waters of Lake Michigan on the Straits of Mackinac, not sitting on an island or peninsula but rising out of the water...*all by itself*. The seventy-six-foot tower was built on submerged shoal at a spot designated key to warn vessels not to wreck on these dangerous rocks. GHOST stories pertaining to this lonely structure say that a worker was killed during the difficult 1847 construction—and his screams can still be heard. Another story said that John Herman, who held the job of lighthouse keeper from 1892 to 1900, was a heavy drinker and fond of playing practical jokes on his assistants. While inebriated he locked one of them up in the tower, a cage-like beacon of distinctive "birdcage" design. Thus imprisoned, the assistant keeper could only watch as Herman tottered along the pier out of sight... never to be seen again. Did John Herman drown? Later keepers told of strange occurrences and noises and doors slamming shut and locking mischievously. They disliked staying at the lighthouse, which needed regular maintenance, bearing as it did the full force of Lake Michigan. When another lighthouse was built at White Shoals nearby, the Waugoshance beacon became less important. It was finally deactivated in 1912.

During World War II, the area was utilized by the United States military for bombing practice and the Waugoshance Shoal Lighthouse was pocked with mortar shells and bullet holes, and gutted by fire and vandalism. Tales continued to circulate of Herman's ghost, "Wobbleshanks" (a corruption of the name of the shoal, also applied to the lighthouse itself). Recently a Great Lakes adventurer named Jack Edwards wrote a narrative in which he and a boating buddy moored at the lighthouse to spend a summer night there—and, hopefully, catch a glimpse of Wobbleshanks. They even brought a bottle of scotch in John Herman's honor. When nothing happened during the dark hours, the discouraged pair departed, but left the scotch and a cooler behind. A short time later they returned. The scotch was apparently untouched—yet, upon uncorking the bottle, Edwards discovered the liquor had been replaced with water! A dead fish also lay rotting in the cooler. A prank played by other boaters or vandals, or Wobbleshanks' sense of humor?

Cracked and stripped of its iron sidings and metal staircase, the lighthouse presents a particularly forlorn residence for any reputed haunt. A not-for-profit organization has been formed to try to restore the Waugoshance Shoal Lighthouse to its former glory, and no doubt legends of Wobbleshanks will persist despite (or because of) their efforts.

WEATHER ANOMALIES — Many INDIAN LEGENDS of giant birds, submarine lynxes, and angry gods were used to personify the forces of nature that aboriginal tribes observed over the Great Lakes. It would not be much of an exaggeration to say that the modern science of meteorology has made but little more progress than animism in explaining some of the more exotic and even dangerous caprices of wind and waves. Little understood, for example, is the "white squall"—a sudden tempest that strikes without warning in otherwise placid weather. It can last only a handful of deadly minutes and whip winds up to one hundred miles per hour. White squalls are reported both on the Great Lakes and in the open ocean and may account for a number of vessels that have simply "gone missing."

In the upper atmosphere, "wind shear" is a term to explain a violent gust that disables and even pulls apart luckless aircrafts, though proponents of TRIANGLES and VORTICES prefer more otherworldly causes.

Both in saltwater and, on rare occasion, in the Great Lakes, shore-dwellers have reported a "boiling of the bay," a phenomenon still unexplained. Its possible origins range from geological to UFOS and USOS. It essentially involves the waters of the lakes suddenly churning violently and then subsiding. Inhabitants and boaters of Traverse City, Michigan, would witness an annual *boiling of the bay* each June in Grand Traverse Bay in the late 1800s and early 1900s, though the phenomenon eventually subsided. On a calm summer day in 1913, the British-built 4,453-ton freighter *Leafield* suddenly became battered by seething surface waves on an otherwise calm Lake Superior. A ready explanation was an underwater earthquake. The *Leafield* survived, but would be lost with two sister ships in the infamous November 1913 storm on Superior.

An 1872 report describes the swells of Lake Ontario rising and falling in an unnatural manner on a clear June afternoon, before a gale hit late in the day, perhaps an example of "seiche waves." A seiche is a recognized but puzzling behavior of lake water that has been suggested when small boats like tugs seem to wreck or capsize for no apparent reason. Thought to be spawned by wind working over a vast area, it's a lone wave of great size and strength that comes without warning and without being preceded or followed by large swells. Seiche waves are noted particularly on Lakes Superior and Erie and may provide a possible explanation for the THREE SISTERS.

"Dark Days" are a strange occurrence noted in old meteorological and historical records along the Great Lakes (sometimes in other parts of the world) when the sky simply becomes black during what would otherwise be normal daylight hours. Such a dark day was recorded in Wisconsin, and across on the Canadian border, March 19, 1886. It was as if some ominous, huge mass were moving overhead slowly, from east to west. On October 14, 1780 and again in July 1814 the community of the Bay of Quinte recorded "dark days," in which the sun disappeared for ten-minute intervals starting at noon. Black clouds with curious yellow streaks scudded through the sky, and there were high winds, thunder, lightning, black rain, and showers of ashes. When the sun did reappear, it seemed blood red.

Yet another bizarre aerial phenomenon of Lake Michigan occurred in late October 1881. Several Wisconsin shore communities, including Milwaukee, Sheboygan, and Green Bay, were covered with cobweb-like strands that drifted down the sky. Charles Fort, a writer who enjoyed listing inexplicable climatological events, described the substance as "strong in texture and extremely white." Such falls of "angel hair" has since been immortalized on paper by many other writers in a Fortean vein, at different sites around the world. Some of the more recent cases turned out to be a species of spider whose newly hatched offspring literally ride the winds, parachute-style, with their webs. The Wisconsonians of 1881, however, checked for spiders; they either found none or overlooked the arachnids due to their small size.

A larger variety of Lake Michigan precipitation fell July 12, 1883, as reported by the crew of the tug *Mary McLane*, as she worked just off the Chicago harbor. At about 6 p.m. the crew said large blocks of ice, as big as bricks, began falling out of a cloudless sky and continued for about thirty minutes. The ice was large enough to put dents in the wooden deck. The crewmembers brought a two-pound chunk of ice ashore with them that night, which they stored in the galley icebox, as proof for their strange story.

WELLER'S BEACH (See SPOOK LIGHTS)

WESTERN RESERVE (See "SUNKEN SISTERS")

WHITE LADY (See DURAND EASTMAN PARK)

WHITE RIVER LIGHT STATION — An alleged haunted lighthouse, now a museum in the warm-weather months. It was built to overlook a channel cut from White Lake to Lake Michigan in the late 1800s to accommodate lumber shipping. The government completed construction of the Norman Gothic-style lighthouse in 1876. The first keeper was William Robinson, a former sea captain who had campaigned to make the lighthouse a reality. He raised a family with his wife Sarah on the site, living there for forty-seven years. By age eighty-seven, he was the oldest lighthouse keeper on active duty, and passed the job on to his grandson. The legend states that William Robinson so wished to remain at White River Light that, enfeebled by age and forced into retirement, he died there the very day he was to move out in 1919. Just a year earlier the beacon had been converted from kerosene to electric, and in 1945, the lens was automated. The romantic idea of Robinson—and his wife Sarah—never leaving his favorite place on Earth has nurtured the idea that the pair are benign GHOSTS on the site, still seeing to the maintenance chores. Footsteps have been heard, and one of the museum administrators claimed to have an agreement with Sarah—if a dust rag is left on the display cases, the job will be found mysteriously completed by unseen hands...Sarah's.

Wheel of the *WILLIAM G. MATHER.*

WILLIAM G. MATHER — A 618-foot freighter, built in 1925 in Detroit and long a flagship of the Cleveland Cliffs mining company, named for William Gwinn Mather (1857-1951), the corporation's first president. She remained part of the fleet until her retirement in the 1980s. The ship was saved from the scrap yard and, donated to the Great Lakes Historical Society, converted into a floating museum, permanently at anchor in downtown Cleveland. She is registered an American Society of Mechanical Engineers National Historic Mechanical Engineering Landmark for her engine and propeller design. Guests can tour her four-story engine room, oaken pilothouse, mammoth hold, and, in fair weather, trod the vast deck, which is available for photo shoots, private parties, and special events. GHOST stories about the *Mather* concern doors opening and closing, phantom voices, music and laughter heard by the staff and crew since the ship's retirement from service, and even the apparent throb of the disused engines running. Some visitors reported seeing fleeting dark figures, and those claiming psychic abilities have reported feelings of dread below deck. Nobody has yet made a connection to the alleged spirit haunting the Grand Island North Light, who, according to darkest gossip, met his doom on the orders of the wealthy and powerful Mather.

WILLIAM H. GILCHER (See SUNKEN SISTERS)

WILMETTE (See *EASTLAND* DISASTER)

WINDIGO — Variously spelled "wendigo," this spirit of INDIAN LEGENDS has been interpreted in various ways by the white Europeans, with some recent cryptozoologists (and comic-book writers) even championing it as a tribal classification of "Bigfoot," or the ever-elusive American version of the Himalayan yeti. The windigo is described as a giant humanoid entity, sometimes white in color, of some fifteen feet in stature. Native traditions associate the windigo with the eating of human flesh; the creature was said to possess a voracious appetite and grew in direct proportion to whatever it consumed. Thus, in a vicious dietary circle, the giant became ever more hungry (and larger) with each feeding. People comprised much of its diet.

A German writer named Johann George Kohl, in the 1850s, wrote down much of the windigo legends of the Ojibway in the Minnesota territories. He distinguished a fine line in native thinking between the concept of the windigo as a beast of (more or less) flesh and blood and a condition in which a person behaves like a windigo, when in the throes of hunger, the Indians' eternal "silent enemy." Here the windigo is the very personification of starvation and madness that overtakes famished humans, leading to cannibalism and other blindly desperate acts. Cannibalism especially was considered to be the effect of windigo possession. Kohl recorded cases of Indians who, driven to eating their fellow tribesmen, were thus shunned and commonly slain by the tribe. In one anecdote, though, an alleged windigo-man found a cure via fortuitous conversion to Christianity.

Winter on the Great Lakes, with the scarcity of game to hunt and the isolation of northern islands, was of particular significance to the cycles of the windigo, though the settlement that bears the dubious honor of being dubbed "Windigo Capital of the World" is Kenora, far inland in Ontario. As a last-resort sustenance, the hungry brave or *voyageur* could make a sort of nauseating-tasting porridge from rock lichen. The Indians knew this as "wendigo wahkoonun." (See also ISLE ROYALE)

WOBBLESHANKS (See WAUGOSHANCE SHOAL LIGHTHOUSE)

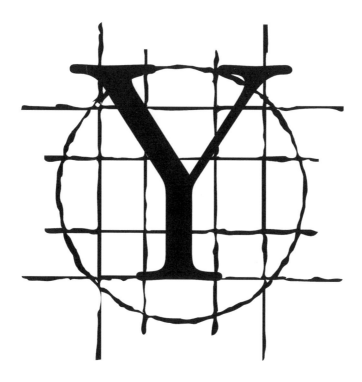

YEO ISLAND — An island in Georgian Bay not far from MANITOULIN ISLAND said to be pranced by a four-footed GHOST in obscure regional lore. In 1828 the British were relocating settlers and livestock from Drummond Island to a new fort. On October 1st, the two schooners involved in the operation ran aground at night at Fitzwilliam Island—the popular accounts state that the liquor carried by a tavern-keeper in transit circulated freely among the crew and contributed to the wreck. The next day the groggy crew, which had managed to escape in a yawl to Yeo Island, came back to the schooner and retrieved remaining survivors, namely the tavern-keeper's wife and daughter and a white saddle horse named Louie, owned by a Drummond Island farmer. Apparently Louie did not so much climb aboard the yawl as was encouraged to ford the waters beside it; when British rescuers came to Yeo Island to take away the marooned civilians and sailors, they determined that their boat was too small to fit Louie in. The white horse was reluctantly abandoned when the castaways departed, and nobody ever mounted a rescue mission for the animal. Yeo Island became known as Horse Island in local parlance, and sailors in later years told of seeing the white steed still on shore, as a phantom.

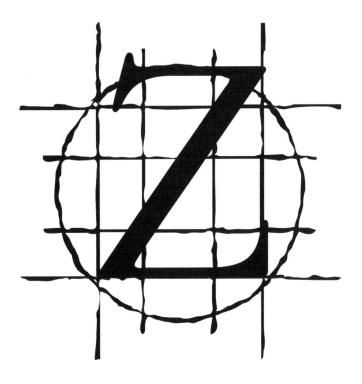

ZEPHYR (See SHIP NAMES)

BIBLIOGRAPHY

Belanger, Jeff. *Encyclopedia of Haunted Places*. Franklin Lakes, New Jersey: New Page Books, 2005.

Berlitz, Charles. *Charles Berlitz' World of Strange Phenomena*. New York, New York: Fawcett Crest, 1968.

Bishop, Hugh. *Haunted Lake Superior*. Duluth, Minnesota: Lake Superior Port Cities, 2003.

Haunted Minnesota. Duluth, Minnesota: Lake Superior Port Cities, 2006.

Bourrie, Mark. *Many a Midnight Ship*. Ann Arbor, Michigan: University of Michigan Press, 2005.

Bowen, Dana Thomas. *Shipwrecks of the Lakes*. Cleveland, Ohio: Lakeside Printing Company, 1952.

Boyer, Dwight. *Ghost Ships of the Great Lakes*. New York, New York: Dodd Mead & Company, 1968.

True Tales of the Great Lakes. New York, New York: Dodd Mead & Company, 1971.

Strange Adventures of the Great Lakes. New York, New York: Dodd Mead & Company, 1974.

Ships and Men of the Great Lakes. New York, New York: Dodd Mead & Company, 1977.

Brinkman, Jim. "Huge steamer simply vanished, She was the '*Edmund Fitzgerald*' of her day." *Leelanau Enterprise*, June 12, 2007.

Cassady, Charles, Jr. *Cleveland Ghosts*. Atglen, Pennsylvania: Schiffer Publishing, Ltd., 2008.

Cochrane, Hugh. *Gateway to Oblivion*. Garden City, New York: Doubleday, 1980.

Columbo, John Robert. *Mysterious Canada*. Garden City, New York: Doubleday, 1988.

Costello, Peter. *In Search of Lake Monsters*. New York, New York: Coward, McCann & Geoghegan, 1974.

Cousineau, Phil. *UFO Secrets Revealed*. New York, New York: Harper Collins, 1995.

Ehle, Jay C. *Cleveland's Harbor*. Kent, Ohio: Kent State University Press, 1996.

Evans, Christopher. "Space Case: The Night the Coast Guard Got Buzzed," *Cleveland Plain Dealer*, July 12, 1992.

Francis, Scott. *Monster Spotter's Guide to North America*. Cincinnati, Ohio: F&W Publications, 2007.

Franklin, Dixie. *Haunts of the Upper Great Lakes*. Holt, Michigan: Thunder Bay Press, 1997

Garrick, David. *Ohio's Ghostly Greats*. Lorain, Ohio: Dayton Lab Press, 1973.

Godfrey, Linda S. *Weird Michigan*. New York, New York: Sterling Publishers, 2006.

Strange Wisconsin: More Badger State Weirdness. Madison, Wisconsin: Trails Books, 2007.

Gordon, Scott. "Waking the Dead," *The Daily Northwestern*, May 7, 2004.

Gourley, Jay. *The Great Lakes Triangle*. Greenwich, Connecticut: Fawcett Publications, 1977.

Guiley, Rosemary Ellen. *Atlas of the Mysterious in North America*. New York, New York: Facts on File, 1995.

Hale, Dennis, Juhl, Tim, Stayer, Pat, and Stayer, Jim. *Sole Survivor*. Lexington, Michigan: Out of the Blue Productions, 1996.

Hauck, Dennis William. *Haunted Places: The National Directory*. New York, New York: Penguin Books, 2002.

Havighurst, Walter. *The Great Lakes Reader*. New York, New York: MacMillan, 1966.

Herguth, Robert C. "Ghost planes plague O'Hare," *Chicago Sun-Times*, May 21, 2000.

Jaworski, Jed. "Revisiting the Mystery of the *W.H. Gilcher*," *Glen Arbor Sun*, August 25, 2005.

Keefe, Bill. *The Five Sisters*. Algonac, Michigan: Reference Publications, 1991.

Kohl, Chris. *Treacherous Waters: Kingston's Shipwrecks*. Chicago, Illinois: Seawolf Publications, 1997.

Shipwreck Tales of the Great Lakes. Chicago, Illinois: Seawolf Publications, 2004.

Lankford, Andrea. *Haunted Hikes*. Santa Monica, California: Santa Monica Press, 2006.

Leise, Cindy. "The Case of the Missing Monster," *Elyria Chronicle-Telegram*, June 12, 2005.

Martin, Jessie A. *The Beginnings and Tales of the Lake Erie Islands*. Detroit, Michigan: Harlo Press, 1990.

McKernan, Lucy. "Set sail early for Halloween haunts," *The Morning Journal of Lorain*, September 26, 2003.

Myers, Arthur. *The Ghostly Gazetteer*. Chicago, Illinois: Contemporary Books, 1990.

Nash, Jay Robert. *Darkest Hours*. Chicago, Illinois: Nelson-Hall, 1976.

Norman, Michael. *Haunted Homeland*. New York, New York: Forge, 2006.

Oleszewski, Wes. *True Tales of Ghosts and Gales*. Gwinn, Michigan: Avery Color Studios, 2003.

Great Lakes Ghost Stories: Haunted Tales Past and Present. Gwinn, Michigan: Avery Color Studios, 2004.

Payerchin, Richard. "Lake Erie monster returns," *Morning Journal of Lorain*, June 12, 2005.

Rath, Jay. *The M Files: True Reports of Minnesota's Unexplained Phenomena*. Madison, Wisconsin: Wisconsin Trails, 1998.

Ratigan, William. *Great Lakes Shipwrecks and Survivals*. Grand Rapids, Michigan: Eerdmans Publishing Company, 1977.

Robinson, Herbert Spencer and Knox Wilson. *Myths and Legends of All Nations*. New York, New York: Bantam Books, 1961.

Sangiacomo, Michael. "'Ghost ship' discovered off Vermilion," *Cleveland Plain Dealer*, June 21, 2007.

Sanderson, Ivan T. *Invisible Residents*. New York, NewYork: Avon Books, 1970.

Schumacher, Michael. *Mighty Fitz: The Sinking of the Edmund Fitzgerald*. New York, New York: Bloomsbury Publishing, 2005.

Scott, Beth and Michael Norman. *Haunted Heartland*. New York, New York: Warner Books, 1986.

Scott, Beth and Norman, Michael. *Haunted America*. New York, New York: Tor Books, 1994.

Spees, Jannifer. *Stranger Than Fiction*. Woodbury, Minnesota: Llewellyn Worldwide, 2002.

Stansfield, Charles. *Haunted Ohio*. Mechanicsburg, Pennsylvania: Stackpole Books, 2008.

Steiger, Brad. *Project Blue Book*. New York, New York: Ballentine Books, 1976.

Real Ghosts, Restless Spirits, and Haunted Places. Detroit, Michigan: Visible Ink Press, 2003.

Stonehouse, Frederick. *Went Missing*. Gwinn, Michigan: Avery Color Studios, 1984 (Revised Edition).

Haunted Lakes. Duluth, Minnesota: Lake Superior Port Cities, 1997.

Haunted Lakes II. Duluth, Minnesota: Lake Superior Port Cities, 2000.

Haunted Lake Huron. Duluth, Minnesota: Lake Superior Port Cities, 2007.

Strand, Ginger. *Inventing Niagara*. New York, New York: Simon & Schuster, 2008.

Stub, Sherry. *Wisconsin Ghosts*. Atglen, Pennysylvania: Schiffer Publishing, Ltd., 2008.

Trickey, Erick. "Wanted: South Bay Bessie," *Cleveland Magazine*, July 2003.

Volgenau, Gerry. *Islands: Great Lakes Stories*. Ann Arbor, Michigan: Ann Arbor Media Group, 2005.

Wachter, Georgann and Michael. *Erie Wrecks West*. Avon Lake, Ohio: Corporate Impact, 2001.

Wachter, Georgann and Michael. *Erie Wrecks East*. Avon Lake, Ohio: Corporate Impact, second revised edition 2003.

Wachter, Georgann and Michael. *Erie Wrecks and Lights*. Avon Lake, Ohio: Corporate Impact, 2007.

Wangemann, Bill. 'Michigan Triangle' To Blame For Weird Occurrences?" *Sheboygan Press*, April 10, 2005.

Webster, Richard. *The Encyclopedia of Superstitions*. Woodbury, Minnesota: Llewellyn Publishing, 2008.

Willis, James A., Henderson, Andrew, and Loren Coleman. *Weird Ohio*. New York, New York: Sterling Publishing Co., 2005.

Woodyard, Chris. *Haunted Ohio*. Dayton, Ohio: Kestrel Publications, 1991.

    Haunted Ohio II. Dayton, Ohio: Kestrel Publications, 1992.

    Haunted Ohio III. Dayton, Ohio: Kestrel Publications, 1995.

    Haunted Ohio IV. Dayton, Ohio: Kestrel Publications, 1997.

    Haunted Ohio V. Dayton, Ohio: Kestrel Publications, 2003.

    Spooky Ohio. Dayton, Ohio: Kestrel Publications, 1995.

Wright, Larry and Patricia. *Great Lakes Lighthouse Encyclopedia*. Erin, Ontario: The Boston Mills Press, 2006.

WEBSITES

www.boatnerd.com
www.christmastreeship.com
www.cleveland.com
www.creepycleveland.blogspot.com
www.deadohio.com
www.hauntedlights.com
www.theshadowlands.net
www.ufocasebook.com
www.waterufo.net

INDEX OF PLACES